Jesus of Nazareth did not write a ⌐ 〔 books written about him. Even people who choose not to believe in him seem unable to ignore him, and often put pen to paper to write about Jesus. However, in *Real Life Jesus* we have something refreshingly different. I found what Mike Cain has written thoroughly engaging, readable, factual, relevant and compelling. The book rings true; it has the marks of authenticity about it. Rarely have I enjoyed a book so much. Not only does it introduce us to Jesus himself, but also to the Gospel of John, and the Bible itself. I realized again just what it is about Jesus, that he remains the defining man of history. I wholeheartedly commend this page-turner to everyone: the convinced will be enthralled, the sceptic will be challenged to rethink, and the indifferent will be stirred.
Roger Carswell, Evangelist

A wonderful blend of rare ingredients: *Real Life Jesus* is conversational in tone, but logical and clear. It taps into our inconsolable longing for wonder and meaning, yet remains light and witty throughout. Most of all, Mike Cain harnesses his zany and fertile imagination to the pulling power of a first-rate biblical worldview. It's a brilliant book and I intend to give one to all those friends of mine who might just give Christianity a second look.
Richard Cunningham, Director UCCF

I defy even the most hardened atheist or the most uninterested agnostic not to be gripped and absorbed immediately by *Real Life Jesus*. From the opening 'tale of the whale' – a metaphor than runs throughout – this book is riveting. We are given the authentic Christ through the first-hand account of our eyewitness (the apostle John), so we are getting back to the original Jesus without any later additions or accretions. At the same time, the Christian message is shown to be totally relevant as it is earthed and applied

to the twenty-first century. Mike Cain has the happy gift of being a wordsmith, so that the book is very arresting and highly readable. But – it is also challenging, so be prepared.
Jonathan Fletcher, Vicar, Emmanuel Church, Wimbledon

In Mike Cain's accessible book, the real Jesus is vividly brought to life from the words of John's Gospel. But *Real Life Jesus* does not leave Jesus in first-century Palestine; it shows how he relates to the kinds of lives many people live today. If you want to discover what sort of relationship you can have with Jesus, this book is for you.
Mike Hill, Bishop of Bristol

For Dad, with love

FOREWORD BY
RICO TICE

MIKE CAIN

Real
Life
Jesus

MEANING, FREEDOM, PURPOSE

ivp

INTER-VARSITY PRESS
Norton Street, Nottingham NG7 3HR, England
Email: ivp@ivpbooks.com
Website: www.ivpbooks.com

First published 2008
Reprinted 2010 (twice)

British Library Cataloguing in Publication Data
A catalogue record for this book is available from the British Library.

ISBN: 978–1–84474–218–9

Set in 12/15pt Adobe Garamond
Typeset in Great Britain by CRB Associates, Potterhanworth, Lincolnshire
Printed in Great Britain by Ashford Colour Press Ltd, Gosport, Hampshire

*Inter-Varsity Press publishes Christian books that are true to the Bible and that
communicate the gospel, develop discipleship and strengthen the church for its
mission in the world.*

*Inter-Varsity Press is closely linked with the Universities and Colleges Christian
Fellowship, a student movement connecting Christian Unions in universities and
colleges throughout Great Britain, and a member movement of the International
Fellowship of Evangelical Students. Website: www.uccf.org.uk*

CONTENTS

FOREWORD

If you read this book you will come face to face with Jesus. Not the Jesus of popular imagination, but the real-life Jesus of history. Not the Jesus of hearsay, but Jesus in his own words, as recorded in the Gospel of John. And there is no-one more important for you to meet.

This is not a dry, preachy book. There is no religiosity, no jargon. You don't need any 'insider' knowledge. Mike approaches the subject as someone who has had his own eyes opened and is longing to share that knowledge. And so his book overflows with warmth and humanity, as he gives us an insight into the life Jesus wants to restore to us. Trusting in Jesus is not about missing out on life. It is about the fullness of life we were created for, the fresh start we all need.

Perhaps you have picked up this book for a friend, longing for them to come to know and trust Jesus. No doubt you are concerned to give them the right material. I can vouch that with this book they will be in safe hands, both in terms of content and approach.

First, and crucially, the Jesus presented here is the Jesus of the Bible. Mike is faithful to John's Gospel throughout. His content is shaped by John's content. And so he is always pointing the reader to the source of information, to the Bible, for it is here in God's word that we find life-changing power.

Secondly, Mike writes out of a love for other people. He has a real heart for his reader, and his desire that they should know the life they were meant for is palpable on every page. And so he beckons them with warmth as well as candour to share with him in the life that can be found only in Jesus. There is no sense of superiority. Instead he builds a natural rapport with his reader, with plenty of down-to-earth illustration from real life that we can all relate to. Above all, here is someone who is delighted to share with others the joy he has found.

And thirdly, Mike is serious in his purpose. He understands the stakes and the urgency of the decision. The strength of his longing for people to put their trust in Jesus informs all that he writes. There is humour, but never flippancy. No attempt is made to soften the importance of a person's response to Jesus.

Or perhaps you have picked up this book as someone indifferent to Jesus. If that's the case, then, with respect, I would say you cannot have really met him. Please may I ask you to let this book make that introduction? Rest assured this won't require you to put your brain to one side. Mike's presentation of Jesus is consistently thoughtful and reasoned. He carefully dismantles the arguments for dismissing Jesus, arguments erected to stave off being confronted with the reality of Jesus. And he shows us that truly to make sense of life and its meaning, it is to Jesus we must go.

I urge you to meet the real-life Jesus in this book. No-one can ignore him for ever.

Rico Tice
Associate Minister, All Souls Church
Langham Place, London

PREFACE

My friends wouldn't say that they were against Jesus. It is more that they don't see why he is relevant to them. That sort of ambivalence has always puzzled me, because, as far as I can tell, the claims Jesus makes about who he is and what he has come to do are compelling. I cannot think of anyone more relevant. As I have talked with my friends, it has often emerged that their knowledge of Jesus has been gleaned from a mixture of religious studies lessons, Christmas carol services and TV documentaries. In our culture Jesus is increasingly marginalized, so it is hardly surprising that our understanding of him is so patchy. But I long for my friends to know that the Jesus they have no time for is a pale imitation of the real Jesus. That is why I have written this book. It is not a technical book and I am aware that it leaves many questions unanswered, but it is an attempt to introduce people to the real Jesus.

I have based each chapter on a section of John's Gospel partly because it was through John's Gospel that my own eyes were first opened to see the real Jesus, and partly because it is my hope that readers of this portrait of Jesus will get a handle on John's much fuller portrait and so be inspired to read John's Gospel for themselves.

ACKNOWLEDGMENTS

If I know anything at all about the real Jesus, it is only because others have patiently answered my questions and taken the time to explain Jesus to me. I owe a great deal to Richard Coekin and Jonathan Fletcher for the way they cared for me in the early years of my Christian life. I have also benefited hugely from hearing sermons on John's Gospel from men such as Don Carson, John Chapman and Mark Ashton. In a way, this book is the fruit of their work. It is full of ideas and illustrations that I have absorbed from them. I am deeply indebted.

I also want to thank John and Anna Smith for the three days of friendship and food in Pembrokeshire during which this book first took shape; Nick and Lucy Pollock for the use of their front room; Al Coffee for his insight; Phil and Christine Mulryne for spurring me on; Richard and Alex Lindley for their thoughtful comments; and Eleanor Trotter at IVP for helping me to go one step at a time. I especially want to thank my family for their patience when I regularly abandoned them at mealtimes in order to race up to my study and scribble down an idea for this book. I want to thank my wife, Clare, for the way she goes on loving me and cheering for me. And I want to thank my children, Tom and Esther, for all the fun we have together.

Chapter 1

A RESCUE STORY

Forty pilot whales lie stranded on Darlington beach, Tasmania. Andrew Irvine, a marine conservation officer, knows that he must act fast.

Scientists are not sure what causes a whale to beach itself. Some have suggested that it is the result of a disease that upsets the mammal's internal navigation system. Herding instincts mean that the whole pod may then follow its disorientated leader into danger. Others believe that the mammals have simply chased their prey too close to the shore and have found themselves trapped in the shallows.

What we do know is that – without intervention – being beached is invariably fatal. Sometimes the whale becomes dehydrated. Sometimes it suffocates as its lungs are crushed under its own body weight, or drowns when the incoming tide covers its blowhole as it lies immobile on its side.

On Darlington beach the huge grey slabs of whale blow and gasp. Several are twitching their fins, and occasionally one will thrash its tail in a desperate bid to right itself. As people arrive on the scene, eager to help, Irvine coordinates the rescue attempt. Someone sets up a hose pump and begins to spray the whales with seawater. Others spread heavy hessian mats over the bodies of the whales and wet them down.

One team of about fifteen people gathers around a large bull pilot whale. The first task is to set the animal upright. Some of the volunteers are in wetsuits; others, in their work clothes, take off their jackets, roll up their trousers and lean their shoulders into the smooth, hard flank of the whale. As though lifting a car on to its side, they eventually heave the whale up and Irvine slides hessian mats under his nose and tail. The team then tries to haul the mats along under the whale's body. Some roll him slowly from side to side. Others scrape away the sand beneath him with hands and spades to get the mats under his middle. When someone brings a spade down by his head the whale flinches, and then falls still. His breathing has become very quiet.

Once the mat is in place, the team begins to drag the whale back towards the sea. On the count of three they lift him for a few metres at a time, then drag and lift and drag until they are waist-deep in water. They push on and soon the whale is floating. But he is very still. Five of the team stay with him to keep him stable. After nearly an hour, he gently flicks his tail and swims off into the ocean. He is back where he belongs.

STRANDED MEN AND WOMEN

The whale was made for the ocean. The ocean is the environment in which it is free to be a whale: to swim, to leap, to sing, to dive down a thousand metres into the dark depths and catch squid with its built-in sonar. It is an awesome creature. On the beach you can still see something of its power and its beauty, but your admiration is mixed with sadness. As it thrashes its tail helplessly, as it lies there limp and wheezing, you know that this was not the life it was created for. A beached whale is a dead whale.

The Bible teaches that, as the whale was made for the ocean, men and women were made for God. He created us to enjoy his love and to reflect his ways on earth. Our relationship with him is, as it were, the environment in which we are free to be fully human. But, as the whale has crashed out of the ocean, humankind has walked out on God. We thought that it would set us free. But it has left us stranded on the beach. Like the whale on the beach, we are noble creatures, but we cannot reflect on our beauty without a sense of sadness.

During the past few days, I have sat by the fire and laughed with friends. I have wandered round an art gallery. I have eaten lamb tagine and lemon syllabub. I have danced around the kitchen table. I have sat spellbound with my children in the theatre and gone with my family for a long and happy walk in the Mendips, when the winter sun shone and the countryside was golden. Life is beautiful. And yet that beauty is shot through with sadness. During the same few days I have wept at the funeral of a friend who committed suicide. Someone else has told me that his marriage is breaking up. The news has been full of the gun crime on our streets, and the body count in the Middle East goes on rising.

The beauty in our world is easy. We don't think twice about what we are to do with it – we just enjoy it. But what are we to do with the sadness?

WHAT ARE WE TO DO WITH OUR SADNESS?
We have been brought up to believe that the story of humankind is a story of progress. In some ways that is true. On the surface, the twenty-first century looks very different from the first century. The world is healthier and wealthier than it has ever been. But under the surface, do you think there is less sadness in the twenty-first century than in the first? Do you think we shed fewer tears? Why is it that we are able to put man on the moon but, despite all the years of technological advancement, we haven't been able to stop him invading other countries, or bullying his friends, or stealing from his neighbour, or walking out on his family? In some parts of the world we may well have extended the average life expectancy by a few years. But when confronted by death we are as helpless and as frightened as we have ever been. For all our progress, we show no sign of being able to eradicate the pain and suffering that blights our world. Whether we are surfing the internet in our high-rise apartment block in Manhattan or lighting a fire outside our tent in the Sahara desert, it makes no difference. Our experience of being human is inextricably bound up with an experience of sadness.

The cheery optimism that says that humankind is on the up and up is a bit like a whale trying to persuade itself that, despite all the evidence, it was made for the beach and that suffocating under its own body weight is as good as it gets. In order to keep up the pretence, the whale has to tell itself that there is in fact no ocean. We have to try to tell ourselves that there is no God.

If there is no ocean, then the whale's experience of the beach is not a problem. It is just how things are. Similarly, if there is no God, then our experience of sadness is not a problem. It is just how things are. If life is just the result of a cosmic roll of the dice, then laughter and tears are neither good nor bad. They are just the numbers that came up. Just as there are mountains and valleys, there is war and there is peace. And just as we wouldn't try to argue that mountains are *morally* better than valleys, a godless universe gives us no grounds for arguing that peace is *morally* better than war. Stuff just happens.

If there is no God, then our experience of sadness is not a problem. It is just how things are.

When we talk about the behaviour of animals, we tend to use the language of instinct and conditioning rather than the language of right and wrong. So we might put down a dog because it had become dangerous, but we wouldn't *blame* it. Because we have been brought up to believe that we are no different from any other animal, when it comes to talking about human behaviour we have tried to use the language of instinct and conditioning rather than the language of moral responsibility. In other words, we have tried to say 'Don't blame me – it was

my genes ... or my upbringing ... or my environment.'
What we do is just what we do. As polar bears hunt seals, so
human beings prey on those who are weak and who stand in
their way.

But it seems to me that there is a tension between the story
we have told ourselves about what it means to be human and
our everyday experience of being human. We say that we are
no more than 'naked apes', yet when someone behaves 'like
an animal', we are quick to identify what they did as being
somehow less than human. In other words, we say that we
are no more than animals and yet, day by day, we expect
people to behave as though they *were* a whole lot more than
animals. Think of how we respond to crime. The fact that
I have no job may form part of the explanation for why I
mugged you, stole your wallet and left you bleeding in the
street. But you would be reluctant to conclude that what I
did was just an instinctive response conditioned by my
environment. You would say that what I did was *wrong*. If I
were to run you down in my car because I was drunk, you
wouldn't be satisfied if the judge in the court dismissed the
case by declaring that my actions were no more than
chemical reactions to external stimulation. You would want
to *blame* me for the choices I had made.

In other words, central to our sense of what it is to be
human is a sense that we are able to make moral choices. In
this, our behaviour is at odds with our beliefs. The logical
conclusion to draw from the story of the universe that we tell
ourselves is that our thoughts and actions are no more than a
series of chemical reactions over which we have no control.
And yet we go on talking about what people *should* do or

ought not to have done as though there is such a thing as an ability to make moral and meaningful choices. But the fact is that the story we have told ourselves about what it means to be human gives us no foundation for our sense of being moral creatures. From where have we smuggled in this sense of morality and meaning?

I am not saying that this proves that there is a God. I am just saying that we find it hard to live in a way that is consistent with our atheism. The story we tell to make sense of what it means to be human doesn't seem to be big enough. So there is a tension at the heart of the human experience. Face down in the sand, all we can see is beach. It is only logical for us to conclude that the beach is all there is. And yet the longing for the ocean won't go away. We're not able just to shrug our shoulders in the face of the sadness and the suffering. We wish that life didn't hurt so much. We campaign against injustice because we think it is wrong, and we weep at the loss of those whom we love. And every time we dream of a better world, we are admitting that human beings are made for something bigger than the beach on which we find ourselves stranded. We are admitting that something has indeed gone wrong.

THE BIBLE MAKES SENSE OF THE TENSION

One of the reasons I take the Bible seriously is because it makes sense of the tension that we feel. The story it tells starts with Genesis. Of course, there is scope for debate on how exactly we are to read the first few chapters. But the author wants us to know that the story of the universe begins with God. It is God who charges the whole universe with

meaning. And we are not just an accidental assortment of
atoms. The Bible says that God made us in his image. In
other words, the Bible has a noble view of humanity and says
that we have been created for a noble purpose. As those
made in the image of God, our purpose is to enjoy his love
and reflect his ways in the world. And life with the Creator,
who made the stars and the dragonflies, is never dull. He
didn't give us fuel to stick into our sides. He gave us food to
taste – like lamb tagine and lemon syllabub. The author of
Genesis says that God looked at all that he had made and
called it 'very good'.

So, on the one hand, the Bible makes sense of the beauty
of life. It says God created this world for us to enjoy. On the
other hand, it also makes sense of the sadness.

The Bible is not an escapist fantasy. It doesn't duck the
hard questions. The Christian God does not call on us to
grin and bear the pain and pretend it isn't there and doesn't
hurt. He wants us to come clean about the ugliness in this
world and the sadness in our lives. He wants us to face up to
the fact that there is a problem, because recognizing that
there is a problem is the first step to a solution. It is like
ignoring a lump in your breast. Pretending that all is well
will only make things worse in the long run.

The Bible says we are right to dream of a better world. As
things stand, this world of ours is *not* as good as it gets. In the
beginning it was good. Very good. But something has gone
wrong. *We* have gone wrong. We have gone wrong because
we have turned our backs on the God who made us.

Our culture is deeply suspicious of any suggestion that *we*
might be in any way to blame for the mess our world is in.

To our ears, it sounds like a sure-fire route to low self-esteem. So to get ourselves off the hook we have pushed God further and further out of the picture. But do you see what has happened? Shrink God, and we end up shrinking all that it means to be human.

The Bible's diagnosis of the human condition may take some chewing on. But you need to know that it does not lead to low self-esteem. Just the opposite. The very fact that we are held responsible underlines the fact that we are not meaningless animals. We are noble creatures, but we have used our nobility badly. Instead of using it to enjoy the God who made us, we have used it to crash out of the ocean. That is why our beauty is shot through with sadness. Stranded on the beach, we thrash about, fighting to eke out some kind of existence. But it's not the life that we were made for. Our days are shot through with death. And our sickness, our frailty and our mortality all point to the fact that we are cut off from the fullness of the life for which we were created, because we have walked out on the God who is the source of life.

JESUS HAS COME TO RESTORE US TO THE LIFE WE WERE CREATED FOR

Towards the end of his account of the life and ministry of Jesus of Nazareth, John, one of Jesus' followers, tells us why he has taken the trouble to write it all up.

> But these are written that you may believe that Jesus is the Christ, the Son of God, and that by believing you may have life in his name. (John 20:31)

In the next chapter we will look at the meaning of words like 'believe' and 'Christ' and 'Son of God'. For now we're just going to concentrate on what John says that Jesus is offering to people like me and you. That phrase 'in his name' means 'on the basis of all that he is and all that he has done'. John is saying that, on the basis of all that Jesus is and all that he has done, dying people like us may have life. In fact, Jesus himself says 'I have come that they may have life, and have it to the full' (10:10).

I think that this comes as something of a shock to us. We have picked up the idea that Jesus came to tie us up in 'thou shalt' knots that are going to restrict our freedom. The word on the street is that he is going to tell us to sit up straight and stop enjoying ourselves: stop thinking, stop feeling, stop laughing. Stop going to the cinema, or making music, or asking questions. We think that following Jesus will mean missing out on life. We think it will mean wearing cardigans and drinking lemon squash from polystyrene cups in the back of musty church halls. We think.

But John says: when you think about what Jesus has come to do, don't think of rules and regulations and rituals. Think of a beached whale being restored to the ocean. Think of it swimming free again.

Jesus goes on to define the 'life' that he has come to bring. On one occasion, when he is praying for his disciples, he says, 'Now this is eternal life: that they [the disciples] may know you, the only true God, and Jesus Christ, whom you have sent' (17:3). He says that the life he has come to bring is about knowing 'the only true God'. In other words, Jesus has come to restore us to the environment for which we were created, because he has come to give us a relationship with the God who made us.

There might be a bit of you that is jumpy about the whole idea of knowing God. We are not sure that we want God looking over our shoulder and breathing down our neck the whole time. It sounds so oppressive. But the ocean doesn't oppress the whale. The deeper it goes into the water, the freer it is to enjoy all that it means to be a whale. God doesn't compromise our humanity. The deeper our relationship with him, the freer we are to enjoy all that it means to be human.

John's big claim is that Jesus has come to restore us to the reason we were put on this planet. He has come to give us the life that we were created for – the life that we long for. Real life.

✣ ✣ ✣

'OK,' you say, 'that's all well and good and everything. I can see how some people might get quite excited about a claim like that. In theory. But it's just not for me.'

Let me put my cards on the table. I want to try to show you that it *is* for you.

Chapter 2

A CLAIM WE CAN'T WALK AWAY FROM
John 20:31

For most people, religion comes under the same category as stamp collecting or Latin American dancing. It is what some people choose to do with their spare time. And, in the same way that not exactly everyone goes for train spotting, not exactly everyone goes for religion. If you do, then we are, on the whole, happy for you. Personally, we can't see the attraction. But then (we find ourselves saying) 'I am not the religious type.'

Fair enough, you might think.

But imagine this. You and I are walking across the Clifton Suspension Bridge in Bristol, admiring the Avon Gorge and peering down at the muddy old river some eighty metres below. After a while, we decide to head down to the towpath. While you make your way back along the bridge,

I stay out in the middle and begin to clamber over the railings. I am just about to step off into thin air when you see what I am up to and yell out, 'Mike, what are you doing?!'

'Well, we wanted to get to the riverbank, so I thought it would be quicker to climb straight down from here,' I explain, in a matter-of-fact sort of way.

'But, Mike, you'll drop straight down into the river. You'll kill yourself!'

'No. Not me,' I reply. 'You see, I am not the gravity type.'

Well, what would you say to that? I take it that you'd tell me in no uncertain terms that, when it came to gravity, my 'type' was irrelevant. You'd tell me that gravity was not just an idea that some people found helpful. Gravity was a reality that everyone in the world needed to reckon with. At least, that's what I hope you'd say.

Our culture has left us with a view of the world in which we would be seriously concerned about the mental well-being of anyone we met who said they were 'not the gravity type', but if we met someone who said they were 'not the religious type' we would barely raise an eyebrow. We have been brought up to believe in two separate worlds. On the one hand there is what we might call the 'physical world', in which we can publicly agree that it is, for example, dangerous to step off suspension bridges. On the other hand there is what we might call the 'spiritual world', which we regard as being essentially private.

Our working assumption is that when people talk about physical things (such as the best route to Middleton-on-Sea), they are talking about something we all need to reckon with. The reason we make a mental note of their suggested route is that we are confident that it will come in handy for us the next time we are heading to the West Sussex coast. But when it comes to someone talking about spiritual things, it is an altogether different story. We have been brought up to believe that when it comes to talking about the route to God, we cannot offer anything more than what we call our 'personal opinion'. By 'personal', we mean 'personal' as in 'personal stereo', as in 'This music is just for me to enjoy.' And just as the music you download and listen to on your iPod reflects your own taste, so the way you talk about God is really just a reflection of your own hopes and hang-ups.

Last week, I had a long conversation over dinner with a woman who told me that she had spent the past three years on a spiritual journey. I asked her if she felt she was approaching any sort of a destination. Had she, for example, found God?

'Oh, no,' she replied. 'But that's not the point. It's the journey that matters, not the destination. This isn't about some god who is out there. This is about getting to know myself better.'

I asked her whether she was following the path of any particular religion.

'What I have done', she explained, 'is I have taken bits from all of them.'

I was intrigued. 'Which bits have you taken?' I asked.

'The bits that resonated with me.'

All the other people who were sitting round the table, pretending not to be listening, nodded sagely. They shared her assumption that religion is an entirely private matter in which I assemble a view of the world that resonates with me.

That's why, when we listen to someone telling us about their spiritual journey, we may well be intrigued – inspired, even – but we don't take notes, because the spiritual Middleton-on-Sea is not a fixed point on the map. It is wherever feels helpful for *you*. They are sharing their experience of the journey, but ours may well be different.

I am not saying that this is how everyone thinks, but it does reflect the way in which many of us think. Just look at the way we bring up our children: when it is a matter of their physical well-being, we insist that they should eat up their broccoli. When it comes to their spiritual well-being, however, we insist that they should be left to find their own way. In the matter of vegetables, we have a very strong sense of what is good for them. When it comes to religion, we are more relaxed.

More important than the fact that I don't want you to walk away is the fact that the claim John makes won't let you walk away.

For as long as we assume that religion is a hobby that is to be stored in a box marked 'Private', we will never hear the claim that John is making in his book. We are liable to flick through his first few chapters and then – thinking we are not the religious type – shrug our shoulders and walk away.

But the thing is, I don't want you to walk away. You need to hear what John is saying. And I say that not as a salesman, but as a beggar who has found a bakery where they are giving away free bread. It is good bread. Without it I would be a dead man. And I don't want you to miss out on this good bread just because you think you are not the religious type.

But more important than the fact that I don't want you to walk away is the fact that the claim John makes won't *let* you walk away. John's book is about Jesus Christ. And here is the thing. John is arguing that Jesus Christ doesn't just give us a way of seeing the world that might resonate with some people. The type of person we are is irrelevant. Like gravity, Jesus Christ is a reality that everyone needs to reckon with.

A CLAIM ABOUT A KING

John has told us that he wants us to read his book so that we can have the life that Jesus brings. To which our question is, 'On what basis does John reckon that Jesus is in any sort of a position to give us this life that he is talking about?' John's answer is in the verse that we looked at in the opening chapter.

> Jesus did many other miraculous signs in the presence of his disciples, which are not recorded in this book. But these are written that you may believe that Jesus is the Christ, the Son of God, and that by believing you may have life in his name. (20:30–31)

The first thing we need to know is that 'Christ' is not Jesus' surname. In first-century Palestine you could not have tracked him down by looking up 'Christ' in the phone book.

'Christ' is a title. It is the Greek for the Hebrew word 'Messiah'. And the Messiah was God's appointed King.

'Son of God' is another phrase used in the Old Testament to denote God's King. The idea was that, in the same way that a son reflects his father (in shape of nose or gift for music), the king of Israel was supposed to reflect God's ways. The Jews were waiting for a Messiah who would be not just another king of Israel, but *the* King, whom God would appoint and who would uniquely reflect the ways of God to a watching world. John's claim is that Jesus is that long-awaited King.

If we are going to make sense of why a two-thousand-year-old claim about a Jewish King should have a hold on our twenty-first-century lives, we will need to look at the claim in the light of God's unfolding plan for his world.

A thumbnail sketch of God's plan

In the previous chapter we saw that the Jewish Bible starts with Genesis. The reason that the Jews believed that their God was the one true God was because he created the whole world. That meant that he was not just their private God, but the God of all people – of all nations. Genesis taught them that when their God made the world he made it good. But it also taught them that something had gone wrong.

Like us, the Jews of Jesus' day were unable to stare blankly at the pain in this world and shrug it all off with 'This is just how things are'. They knew that it shouldn't be like this. And, like us, they longed for things to be put right. Throughout the dark times, they held on to the promises that their God had made near the very beginning of the Bible.

Back in Genesis, God took hold of a man named Abraham and made this promise to him:

> I will make you into a great nation
>   and I will bless you;
> I will make your name great,
>   and you will be a blessing.
> I will bless those who bless you,
>   and whoever curses you I will curse;
> and all peoples on earth
>   will be blessed through you.
> (Genesis 12:2–3)

God promises that through one particular nation (the descendants of Abraham) he will reach out to all nations. Through this one people he will bring 'blessing' to 'all peoples on earth'. The history of Israel is the story of the Creator God working out his plans to keep that promise to put right the world that we have messed up.

As the descendants of Abraham grew into a fully fledged nation, they established a monarchy, and the kings of Israel were meant to rule the nation with the sort of love and justice that reflected the fact that their God was supremely loving and just. But one king after another turned away from the ways of God. Instead of harmony there was division and injustice that tore the kingdom of Israel apart.

But through the prophets God said that one day he would appoint a King, in the line of King David, who would indeed rule with love and justice. This King would be a blessing not only to Israel but to all people of all nations, because he would rule over not only Israel but the whole world and would unite all nations in a kingdom of peace and harmony.

At the time of Jesus, there was the particular hope that the coming of the King to put things right would mean dealing with the Romans. They had occupied the land of the Jews and seemed to be responsible for much of what was going wrong in the world. But the vision of the prophets pointed to something bigger than regime change: it pointed to a whole new order of creation. It is a vision that reaches its climax towards the end of the Bible.

> Then I saw a new heaven and a new earth, for the first heaven and the first earth had passed away, and there was no longer any sea . . . And I heard a loud voice from the throne saying, 'Now the dwelling of God is with men, and he will live with them. They will be his people, and God himself will be with them and be their God. He will wipe every tear from their eyes. There will be no more death or mourning or crying or pain, for the old order of things has passed away.' (Revelation 21:1–4)

Where is God's plan heading?

The people in the Bible long with all their hearts for this new world. It is what keeps them going through the dark days. But it is hard for us to share their enthusiasm. That is because, if we think of life beyond the grave at all, we tend to think of it as a flimsy disembodied sort of an existence, floating around in a kind of cloudland. And, however hard we try, we cannot pretend that is an appealing prospect. If you worry that we are going to have to sit through endless choir practice wearing nothing but a Laura Ashley nightdress, you need to know that the popular picture of the afterlife is not one we get from the Bible.

The world to come will not be a ghostly imitation of the world we live in now. It will be this flesh-and-blood world restored to all the glory for which it was originally created. In other words, it will be *more* real, not *less* real. *This* is the flimsy world, where things fade and wither and spoil and die. In the new world our joys will be *more* solid, our pleasure *more* substantial.

And it will *not* be boring. Our lives *today* are marked by boredom and disappointment, but in the new world we will finally know what it is to be satisfied. And in the new world there will be no more 'mourning or crying or pain' because there will be no more death, because we will be restored to the God of life. All that has gone wrong in this world will be put right. So it is not 'the afterlife', like an afterthought tacked on at the end. It is the destination to which God's promises to Abraham have all been heading. It is the main event.

In the new world we will finally know what it is to be satisfied.

The Bible calls it 'home'. Home is not just the place where you can rest after a long hard day. Being at home is about being in the place where you belong. It is where you are free to be yourself because you feel safe, and you feel safe because you feel loved. The Bible says that in this world we are a long way from home, which is why we often feel so lost and lonely, and sometimes even the houses we live in don't feel much like the home we long for. The reason that the people in the Bible longed for God's King to come was that he was the one through whom God was going to lead them home.

The coming of God's King

But the Old Testament ends with the people still waiting. Eventually, four hundred years after the last of the Old Testament prophets, John the Baptist starts preaching in the desert. Thousands flock to hear him. He tells everyone to get ready, because the one they have been waiting for is coming. And then one day, by the river Jordan, John the Baptist points to a carpenter's son from Nazareth and cries out, 'There he is! The one we have been waiting for has come.'

Do you see what is at stake here? For the moment I am not making a case for the *truth* of John's claim. I am making a case for the *type* of claim that he is making.

Imagine I live on the eighth floor of a block of grey concrete flats. One day you come and visit me. After climbing the eight flights of stairs you walk through my door and, still catching your breath, mutter something like, 'Blocks of flats like this ought to be blown up!' How am I to respond? Well, although I might be a bit offended (it is, after all, my home you are talking about), I don't for one moment think to call the emergency services and warn them of an impending attack. You have articulated an idea. You have merely expressed your dislike of my flat in graphic terms.

You are free to do this. And I am free to ignore it and get on with making you a cup of coffee.

But if there was a pounding on my front door and I opened it to a yellow-helmeted fireman, who with great urgency informed me that someone had planted a bomb in the building, then my response would be very different. If I responded with 'That's an interesting idea, but I am not the sort of person who thinks flats like this should be blown up' and then went back to my supper, I think you would understand the fireman's frustration. It may turn out to be a false alarm, but if someone claims that the building I am in is about to be blown up, that is a claim I need to reckon with.

When it comes to Jesus, John is not making an 'I think your flat should be blown up' sort of claim. He is not presenting Jesus as merely an idea that some people might find helpful and others might find offensive. What he is saying is that the one true God who created this world has been unfolding his plan to put this whole world right. And now, through Jesus, he is bringing that plan to its climax. If you were in a building in which there was a bomb scare, you would at least need to reckon with it, if only to establish that it was a false alarm. If you are in this world, then John's claim is one that you need to reckon with. Upon investigation, you might decide that it is a false alarm. But you cannot dismiss it as an idea that doesn't resonate with you. It is not that sort of claim.

WHAT ARE WE TO DO WITH THIS CLAIM ABOUT A KING?

John tells us the kind of response he is looking for.

Faith in the King

These are written that you may believe. (20:31)

'Believe' is the verb of which 'faith' is the noun. In other
words, John has written his Gospel so that we put our faith in
Jesus. Faith is about trust. The fireman at my door is asking
me to put my faith in him. I *could* respond to him by saying
that I thought there was a lot of truth in what he was saying,
and that I was very impressed by his bravery and was
determined to become a braver man myself ... and then
return to my supper. But that would not be the sort of
response he was looking for. The fireman wants me to trust
him. That will mean taking him at his word, putting my life
in his hands and letting him lead me down the stairs to safety.

Jesus doesn't want us just to agree with some of his
teaching, or be inspired by his example. He came to lift us
off the beach and put us back in the ocean. Jesus wants us to
trust him. That will mean taking him at his word, putting
my life in his hands and letting him lead me back to God.
That is what it means to have faith in him.

Faith is about looking at the evidence, not leaping in the dark

The trouble is, we have been brought up to believe that just
as physical claims are public and spiritual claims are private,
so faith in the fact that an aeroplane can fly is rational but
faith in God is inherently *ir*rational. I have always been
puzzled by this. It seems to me that the sort of people who
write letters to the newspapers saying that, in the name of

rationality, we should banish God from public discourse are in fact sawing off the branch they are sitting on. If there is no God, then the universe is ultimately an irrational kind of place and you and I are ultimately an irrational kind of animal, driven more by impulse than by reason. God is not the enemy of rational thought. He is its foundation.

Because God is rational, weighing up the claim that he makes on our lives calls for a rational response. Please don't misunderstand me here. I don't mean that faith is about coming up with a theory of God that fits in with our idea of what we think God should reasonably be like. The God of the Bible is not an invention of the philosophers. He is there, and he is bigger than our small minds and so will constantly challenge the small ways in which we think. But the point is that, when it

God is not the enemy of rational thought. He is its foundation.

comes to weighing up his claim on our lives, he is *not* asking us to unscrew our brains.

The kind of thing my friends who are not Christians say is: 'I'd love to believe like you do, but I just don't have the faith.' As though faith is a knack for credulity that some people are born with and others aren't, like an eye for a ball or an ear for a tune.

The most important thing about faith is its object. Imagine that you and I are standing together on the edge of a frozen pond. We'd both love to go skating on it. You have absolute faith that the ice is thick enough. I am not so sure. You tell me that I just need to have faith. After a moment's hesitation we both step onto the ice. Which of us will the ice hold up? It is, of course, an illogical question. Either the ice is thick enough to hold us both, or it is too thin to hold either of us. The issue is not how much faith each of us has, but how thick the ice is.

But in today's spiritual landscape, people tend to focus not so much on the object of faith (the ice) as on faith itself (your belief that the ice could hold you up). So you may think that John is asking you to do an impossible thing, because you may imagine that he is calling you to drum up a faith that you simply don't possess. But all the faith in the world won't make the ice hold me up if it isn't thick enough.

That is why John is *not* calling you to drum up more faith. He is trying to persuade you that the ice is thick enough. He wants to show you that if you stand on Christ, Christ will not crack.

In the face of the fireman's claim, I would look for signs that I could trust him. Does he look like a real fireman? Is he wearing a badge? Is there a fire engine down below? Can I hear sirens? Does the evidence stack up? John is not asking us to respond to Jesus as a poet might ask us to respond to his poem. He is making a claim that is rooted in events that happened in history and he wants us to weigh up these events. John was one of Jesus' closest friends. In the verse that we looked at earlier, he says he has written a book of 'signs'. In other words, he has gathered together some of the things that he saw Jesus do and heard him say. He has lined his material up like a row of witnesses in a law court and, as we read, he wants us to ask ourselves whether the evidence stacks up.

John wants to show us that Jesus is not just an idea that some people may find helpful. Jesus has a gravity-like claim on us all. And as we consider that claim, John is not asking us to emulate the White Queen, whom Alice encountered in *Through the Looking-Glass*, and make ourselves believe 'six impossible things before breakfast'. He is saying: 'Look at the signs. What direction do they point in? Does Jesus look like God's King, come to put things right and make the whole world new again?'

In this book there isn't the space to work through all of John's material, so we are going to zoom in on key bits of the evidence that he has collected. We will focus on his presentation of Jesus as the one who can give us 'life in all its fullness'. Along the way we will be asking: why does John think that Jesus is the one who can give us the life that we were created for? Why is this life worth having? How does Jesus give it to us?

✛ ✛ ✛

It may be that you understand perfectly well the type of claim that John is making, but the reason why you are not interested in pursuing it is because of your suspicions about the type of God that John is talking about. It is as if someone has offered you an evening's fishing on an exclusive stretch of the River Test. You understand the offer, but you don't take it up because, frankly, you can't think of a more tedious way to spend an evening. In the next chapter we shall see that the God of the Bible is not like we sometimes think he is.

Chapter 3

GOD HAS A FACE
John 1:1–18

For many of us, God is like the Loch Ness Monster. Some people claim to have caught glimpses of him. But when you compare their stories, it turns out that they all have slightly different ideas about what they think they've seen. Devotees have trawled the Loch with submarines and sonar equipment. Miles of film have been shot and thousands of photographs have been taken in countless attempts to capture conclusive proof of the monster's existence. But all we have to go on are a few grainy pictures that are just enough to keep our hopes up. There's no *proof* that it exists. But then, hey, there's no proof that it doesn't. So people go on searching. And so it is with God. Most of us are open to the idea that there may well be someone out there, lurking in the darkest depths of the universe. We are curious about him in much the same way that an adopted child is curious about its biological parents. We think that if we understood more about him, it might help us to understand more about ourselves. It might help us to fit some of the pieces together. But after years of searching, we are with the philosophers on this one: even if there is a God, we can't know him. Not really. Once in a while we may stumble across a footprint, or think we see a flash of a tail. We may have some kind of spiritual experience that keeps our hopes up. But, like the Loch Ness Monster, God seems to be keeping himself to himself.

In the previous chapter we saw that John's claim is that the God of the Bible is not merely the hopes and fears of a particular group of people projected onto a large religious screen. His claim is that there is a God who really is out there. But even that doesn't swing it for us.

And we want to know why God doesn't seem to care.

We are people who have been caught up in the crossfire of family break-up. We have had to stand by the graves of people we have loved. We have known what it is to be surrounded by a whole hatful of friends and still feel terribly alone. We have seen the poverty in Africa and watched footage of the bloodshed in the Middle East. And we want to know why God doesn't seem to care. Maybe, when we were younger, it was comforting to believe that there was a God out there, somewhere, watching over us. But not any more. Now that we have lived a little, we want to know where he was when his world needed him. If he cared, you'd think he would come out of hiding. You'd think he'd do something to fix things. But the fact is that he doesn't seem all that bothered about us. And that makes it hard for us to feel all that bothered about him.

So, yes, we might believe that there is a God. Out there. Somewhere. But what good is a God who sits out there beyond the stars, when I have a knot in my stomach on a Monday morning?

I often meet people who have no time for God. But, more often than not, it transpires that the God they have no time for is not the God of the Bible. The God they don't believe in is one I don't believe in either. The God of the Bible is not the god within. He is not merely the projection of our hopes and fears. He is the God who is really out there. But he is no Loch Ness Monster. The good news is that God is there and he is not hiding.

THE GOD WHO HAS COME CLOSE TO US

You move into a new flat. As far as you understand it, the flat above yours is empty. But, every so often, you are sure that you hear footsteps overhead. You regularly nip upstairs and ring the bell, with the intention of introducing yourself to your neighbour. But no one ever answers the door.

Then one day you notice that on the main door downstairs a name has appeared by the bell for the flat above you. 'Alex Jones', it says. That confirms your suspicions. There *is* someone in the flat above.

As you climb the stairs you can't help but wonder what this Alex Jones is like. In your mind she sounds like the sort of person who is tall, has long red hair and wears glasses. Then one afternoon there is a knock on your door. 'Hello,

I am from the flat above. I've just moved in. I thought I'd come and introduce myself.' It turns out that Alex Jones is short and chubby and has a goatee beard. His mates call him Al.

The Alex Jones of your speculation was always going to be way off the mark. The only way to arrive at the truth about Alex Jones was for Alex Jones to come knocking on your door. And so it is with God.

Sometimes we hear his footsteps. When we look up with wonder at the stars on a frosty night. Or when we are driving and a piece of music on the radio is so beautiful that we have to stop the car and just listen. Or when we are overwhelmed with love for someone. Like footsteps in the flat above, they make us wonder if there is – despite what we have been told – someone out there after all. But when it comes to arriving at the truth of what that someone might be like, our only hope is for him to come and make himself known to us.

John is telling us that that is exactly what has happened. He sums this up in four words. They are four words that changed my life, because they showed me that the God of the Bible was not how I had imagined God to be. He is not 'out there' somewhere beyond the stars, paring his fingernails and looking down at us with indifference. In Jesus Christ the God who is out there has come knocking on our door.

John says, 'The Word became flesh' (1:14). He calls Jesus 'the Word'. He does it to make a point. In the Bible God's 'Word' is how he makes himself known. If you and I were to meet at a party, in order to get to know you I would listen to your words. You might tell me that you were from

Barnstaple, that you liked gangster films and were studying to be a vet. If you never said a word, I would not know who you were. I would just have to guess. John is saying that God has not left us guessing about what he is like. Jesus Christ is the Word that he has spoken.

There's a temptation to take this in our stride and think of Jesus as just another prophetic voice in a long line of religious leaders who claim to have caught a glimpse of God. But John stops us in our tracks. Look at what he says about this 'Word'. This is how he starts his Gospel:

> In the beginning was the Word, and the Word was with God, and the Word was God. He was with God in the beginning. (1:1–2)

What John is telling us is that the story of Jesus did not begin in Bethlehem. In the beginning, when the world was first created, Jesus was there. He was there 'with God'. The phrase John uses implies more than just that Jesus was present. He was 'with God' in the sense that he was in a loving relationship with God. And we have to catch our breath. What sort of a person was in a loving relationship with God from the beginning? John goes on: 'and the Word was God.' There is our answer. The sort of person who was in a loving relationship with God from the beginning is the sort of person who is in fact God. John continues:

> Through him [that is, through this Word] all things were made; without him nothing was made that has been made. (1:3)

The Word was not just with God from the beginning, watching, as it were. It was through him that God made the whole universe. So, when John says that Jesus is the 'Word' who 'became flesh', he is claiming that before Jesus was born as a baby he was in fact something else. He was the eternal Word of God, eternally with God, eternally God. And then there came a moment in time, during the reign of Caesar Augustus, when the one who made the stars *became* a tiny dividing cell in the womb of an unmarried Jewish girl and was born on a stable floor in a small village just a few miles south of Jerusalem. If you had been one of the shepherds looking at this baby, you would have been looking into the face of God.

Jesus is not just a God enthusiast pointing to the possibility of God's existence. Jesus is God come knocking on our door. That may be more than you are willing to take on board right now. But, if you are going to weigh John's evidence, you will at least need to hold on to that idea. It is at the heart of the claim that he is making.

The fact that Jesus is God come close to us shows us two things about what God is really like: that he is committed to his creation and that he is committed to a relationship with us.

God is committed to his creation

If you think God doesn't care much for what happens in this world, then you will think that being a Christian means you shouldn't care very much about what happens in it either. You won't vote and you won't go to the theatre. But here is the thing: God *does* care. He created this world. And when

he created it he said that it was 'good'. Yes, something has
gone very wrong. We have walked out on God. But *he*
has not walked out on us. The Creator is committed to his
creation. 'In the beginning' is a deliberate echo of the
opening words of the Bible. The story of the world begins
with the Creator. And John is saying that here is a new
beginning for our world. And it too begins with the Creator.
Because he is committed to his creation, he has come to put
this broken world back together again.

God is committed to a relationship with us

John is telling us that there is one God, but he is made up of
more than one person (three persons, in fact). This is not the
moment to explain what theologians call 'the doctrine of
the Trinity'. The point to hold onto for now is that the God
of the Bible is nothing like the philosophers imagine him to
be. We can harness the power of the wind, but we can't have
a loving relationship with it. John wants us to know that the
God of the Bible is not a force that we can harness; he is a
person whom we can love. In fact, he is three persons in
relationship. In other words, relationship is at the very heart
of who he is. This God is not a lonesome cowboy of a god
who lies low in the margins of the universe, avoiding us
because he doesn't do relationships. Relationship is what he
is all about. Let's look again at chapter 1, verse 14. John goes
on to say that the Word 'made his dwelling among us'.
Literally, John says that he 'tabernacled' with us. John is full
of Old Testament echoes. The tabernacle was the tent that
God told Moses to make when the Israelites were fleeing
from Egypt through the desert. It was to be pitched in the

centre of the camp as a symbolic reminder that their God was not a faraway sort of a God, but the God who comes close to his people and lives among them. John is saying that the tabernacle was a symbol that pointed forward to Jesus. In the coming of Jesus, God himself has come close to us. God wants us to have more than just a sense that there might be someone out there. He is the God of relationship and he has come because he wants us to have a relationship with him.

This turns on its head all that we think about God. We think religion is about people who have set off on a long search for a god who is hiding. But in the Bible there is no parable of the lost shepherd being tracked down by the conscientious sheep. The Christian claim is that it is all the other way round. We have got ourselves badly lost, and it is God who has come looking for us. And when he comes, he comes to us not as a force that we are to harness, but with a face that we are to love.

This is good news for our world. John talks about the coming of the Word into the world as the coming of light into darkness. We are only too aware of being in the dark. We are not sure of who we are, why we are here, or where we are going. But the God who made us has come to bring light into our darkness. He has come to make sense of our lives. If there is anyone who could give us the answers we long for, it has got to be him.

Only it's not always very easy to pluck up the courage to ask a question of someone who knows everything. At school I found maths a little slippery. I had a teacher who was brilliant at it. As far as I could tell, he knew everything there was to know about maths. But that was why I found it so hard. I didn't have the nerve to stick up my hand and ask questions, because I wasn't sure that he understood the struggles I was having. I thought that as it all came so easily to him he'd think my questions were foolish.

When it comes to God, we can feel a similar thing. He may well be the one with all the answers – technically. But we don't feel we can turn to him with the questions on our hearts, because – well – what would he know of the struggles we face to survive in this world of his? What would *he* know about what it felt like when they all laughed at me? Or when I failed my exams? Or when she broke my heart?

THE GOD WHO BECAME ONE OF US

When God comes with answers, he doesn't just give us an earful of words. He becomes one of us.

If John had said that the Word 'became a human being', that would have been pretty startling to his first readers. But this word 'flesh' is more than startling. It is almost crude. He is rubbing his readers' noses in what's happened.

And the reason why we need our noses rubbed in it today is because we have seen so many paintings of Jesus floating around Jerusalem pale as a ghost and with a large yellow dinner plate stuck to the back of his head. It is often great painting, but it's not such great theology, because it makes Jesus seem less than human. And the less human he seems, the less likely we are to want to turn to him with our questions.

John says, 'I'm talking about a God who became flesh.' Flesh gets tired and hungry. It aches. You see, God didn't come and *play* at being a man. He stood right up to his neck in what it means to be a man. He became a refugee. He was mocked by his own family. He was found guilty by an establishment that wanted rid of him. By the grave of a friend called Lazarus, Jesus wept real tears. In the garden of Gethsemane, the night that he was betrayed, that was real sweat on his brow. When they nailed him to the cross, it was real blood that he shed.

The point is that God became *one of us*.

In 1863 a Catholic priest by the name of Father Joseph Damian was inspired by the example of Jesus to go to help a leper colony on one of the Hawaiian Islands. The people there had been banished without family, friends or any sort of help. Father Damian went to live among them. He buried the dead, cleaned the water system, built them homes and set up a school, a hospital and two church buildings. In 1885 the lepers were stunned when he started a sermon one Sunday with the words 'We lepers...' He too had contracted the disease.

This man was prepared to go to those lepers and show them love, even though it meant becoming one of them. And that is what God has done for us. It may be that you think that God is out there, but you've never had the nerve to turn to him with your questions because you're not sure that he would know what it feels like to be you. But when Jesus – the one by whom the world was made – speaks to us, he says 'We humans...'

Are you misunderstood by the people closest to you? He has been there. Are you grieving? He has cried by the grave of a friend. Have friends let you down? He knows how it feels to be betrayed. Are you close to giving up? He knows exactly what you are going through. It is not just that he knows everything about you because he made you. He knows everything about you because he knows what it feels like to *be* you.

Taking in John's four words ('the Word became flesh') changes not just everything we ever thought about God, but everything we ever thought about what it means to be human. We place our feet firmly in the soil and run the earth over our toes and know for sure that the world is physical and that our own physicality is fundamental to what it means to be human. Yet, as we survey the landscape and watch the trees bending in the wind, we are blown away by the beauty of it and we know for sure that there is so much more to it all. We know that we are both physical and spiritual beings, yet we are not sure how to fit those two realities together. Somewhere along the line we have made a connection between being spiritual and going without food, or abstaining from sex, or not playing sport on Sundays. Our suspicion is that physicality and spirituality do not mix, and that we must all choose one at the expense of the other. That is why we fear that turning to Christ will mean we become less engaged with the real world of essay deadlines, job interviews, mortgages and football teams.

But Christianity that is truly rooted in Christ will never lead to spiritual escapism. Look at the sort of God that Christ makes known to us. Not only did he create the physical world and call it 'good'. He entered into it. 'The Word became flesh.' This is not a God who is calling us to shrug off our physicality – this is a God who took on our physicality.

In Christ we see how the two halves of our human experience come together: we see that the more we engage in what it means to be spiritual, the more we will engage in what it means to be physical. The more I engage with the God who made this planet, the more I will know how to live on this planet. Look at him. He didn't turn his back on this world. He cares so much about this world that he rolled up his sleeves and stepped into the thick of it. And following him means we are set free to do the same.

Deep down, we fear that living for God will make us less human. We touched on that in chapter 1, but here we see more. We see Jesus. When God comes to show us what he is like, he comes as man. The one who is fully divine walked this planet as the most fully human being this world has ever seen. It turns out that God knows more about being human than I do. And if I knew more of God, I would know more of what it means to be a human.

Christianity that is truly rooted in Christ will never lead to spiritual escapism.

THE GOD WHO HAS COME TO OUR RESCUE

It's not just that in Christ God has shown us the truth. In Christ he has come to our rescue. And rescuing us means restoring us to the relationship with him for which we were created. It's a theme that John develops during the course of his book. But he launches it here in the opening chapter. He says:

> To all who received him, to those who believed in his name, he gave the right to become children of God. (1:12)

Jesus came to give us the right to become children of God. In other words, the reason we need rescuing is because, without him, we *don't have that right*.

What John is saying is that our fundamental human problem is that we have not lived as God's children. We have crashed out of the relationship with God for which we were made. And, like beached whales, it is not just philosophical problems we've got. It is life problems. We need more than answers to our big questions. We need someone to restore us to the environment for which we were created.

Think back to Andrew Irvine and his team of rescuers. They didn't just sit back and watch the whales' plight from a distance. Their commitment to the whales meant they rolled up their sleeves and went down onto the beach and stood alongside them. But their commitment didn't stop at standing alongside them. They didn't just go and tell the whales about the ocean. They restored them to the ocean.

And that is what Jesus has come to do for us. He hasn't just come to stand alongside us in order to *tell* us about the reason we were created. He has come to *restore* us to the reason we were created. 'In him was life' (1:4), says John. And he has come to give us the life that we need, to restore us to the relationship with God that we were created for.

John will go on to tell us more of *how* Jesus restores us to God. But in this opening chapter he is already preparing the ground.

THE BRILLIANCE OF GOD

John says 'The Word became flesh and made his dwelling among us,' and he continues: 'We have seen his glory, the glory of the One and Only, who came from the Father, full of grace and truth' (1:14).

We sometimes say to someone, 'Go on, then. Show us what you're made of!' We are asking that person to show us their 'glory', to show us what they are like in all their brilliance. God's 'glory' is what God is like in all his brilliance. But in Old Testament times no one could look on God's glory and live. It would have been like standing too close to the sun. On the famous occasion when God showed Moses his glory, we read that he 'passed by'. If God had shown him his face, Moses would have died. So he just gave him a glimpse of his back, as it were.

John is saying that in Jesus Christ God has made it possible for us to see his glory.

> No-one has ever seen God, but God the One and Only, who is at the Father's side, has made him known. (1:18)

In Jesus we don't just catch a glimpse of God – see footprints or the flash of a tail – we can look into his face and see God in all his brilliance.

Only it is not the sort of brilliance we might have in mind. Jesus goes on to speak of the 'hour of his glory'. He tells his disciples that there will come a crowning moment when his brilliance will be displayed for all to see. When I think of an 'hour of glory', I think of winning the World Cup, or going up for an Oscar, or being presented with a Nobel Prize. But here is the thing: Jesus goes on to say that his hour of glory is the hour of his death.

Restoring whales to the ocean took hose pumps and hessian mats. It turns out that restoring us to God took the death of Jesus on a cross. It is there that we see God in all his brilliance, for it is there that we see what it meant for him to come and restore us to the reason for which we were created.

This turns everything we have thought about God upside down and inside out. How can crucifixion reveal the brilliance of God? It may reveal the brutality of this world, but surely not the brilliance of God? The whole idea seems so twisted. But John insists that in Jesus we see the brilliance of God, a brilliance that reaches its climax on the cross. In other words, John is saying, 'If you don't think much of God, look at Jesus. Listen to what he says. Watch what he does. Keep watching all the way to his death on the cross. Because it is then, when you see what he has done to rescue you, that you will see just how brilliant he is.'

> The Word became flesh and made his dwelling among us. We have seen his glory, the glory of the One and Only, who came from the Father, full of grace and truth.' (1:14)

It is the cross that will show us just how 'full of grace and truth' he is.

Perhaps you think of God as cold and uncaring. It is as we understand the cross that we see that he is full of grace. He doesn't leave us in the mess we have got ourselves into. He loves us so much that he comes to us as a man like us – not just to live our life, but to die our death. We have done nothing to deserve it. But he does it anyway. Because he is full of grace.

Perhaps you think that God has let you down. It is as we understand the cross that we see that he is 'full of truth', in the sense of being 'true to someone'. In other words, he is faithful. He keeps the promise he made to Abraham and comes after us to make a new start. The cross shows us how much it cost him to keep that promise. But still he kept it. He is full of truth.

In the previous chapter we thought about the type of claim John is making. In this chapter we have been looking at the type of God John is talking about. He is no Loch Ness Monster, hiding from us. This is the God who has come looking for us, because he loves us and wants to restore us to the relationship with him for which we were made. To track us down cost him everything. But that is the type of God he is.

✢ ✢ ✢

I remember exactly where I was on the day I first understood that God was not as I had imagined him to be. When I saw how good he was, I wanted to know more. If he had come to give me the right to be his child, then I desperately wanted to have him as my Father. And I remember asking a friend of mine how to go about starting out on this new life with God. His answer was along the lines of what Jesus says to a man called Nicodemus, whom we are about to meet.

Chapter 4

A FRESH START
John 3:1–21

Meet Nicodemus.

> Now there was a man of the Pharisees named Nicodemus, a member of the Jewish ruling council. He came to Jesus at night...' (3:1–2)

Nicodemus is a Pharisee, which means he is one of about 6,000 Jewish people who have taken a public vow to devote their lives to religion. He is also a member of the Jewish ruling council, and Jesus describes him as 'Israel's teacher'. He is something like a bishop, an MP and a professor of theology all rolled into one. I imagine that his mother is very proud of him indeed.

If Nicodemus were to go on *Mastermind*, his chosen subject would be 'The kingdom of God'. As we have seen, the Jews believed that through them the God who created the world was fulfilling his plan to set up his eternal kingdom.

In the back of our minds alarm bells are ringing. As far as we can tell, when anyone gets it into their head to set up their kingdom there will be tanks in the streets and men and women disappearing in the middle of the night. We can't help but be suspicious of God's motives. But Nicodemus yearns for the kingdom of God, because he knows how good it will be. He knows that the Creator's plan to bring all things back under his rule is not a plan to oppress people, but to set them free – to restore the whale to the ocean. As Nicodemus makes his way through the streets of Jerusalem, it is the prospect of that day that quickens his steps towards Jesus.

The prophets had said that the King through whom God would set up his kingdom would heal the sick, give sight to the blind and make the lame walk. Those were the kinds of miracle that Nicodemus had seen Jesus performing. And he knew that they weren't just party tricks to impress the crowd. They were signs. And he thought he saw the direction in which these signs were pointing: here was Jesus putting broken lives back together again. Could he be the one through whom God was going to put the whole broken world back together? There was a rumour that, at a recent wedding in Cana, Jesus had turned water into wine (2:1–11). Nicodemus knew from the Old Testament that 'new wine' was one of the prophets' favourite images to describe the richness of life in the kingdom of God. Was this the King who would bring the life that they had been longing for?

In Nicodemus' mind the stakes are very high. He is not going to Jesus just to explore his own spirituality. He is going because, when God puts this broken world back together and makes all things new, he wants to be part of it. He does not want to miss out. And for us the stakes are the same. How do you and I get to be part of the kingdom of God?

Notice that Nicodemus goes to Jesus 'at night'. Maybe he didn't want everyone to know that he, the learned and highly respected Nicodemus, was off to take advice from this maverick carpenter from Nazareth. Maybe John draws attention to the fact that it was night to make the point that – for all his theological expertise – when it came to the question of how you get into the kingdom of God, Nicodemus was well and truly in the dark.

The first thing that Jesus says to Nicodemus is that to get into the kingdom of God you need a miracle.

TO GET INTO THE KINGDOM OF GOD YOU NEED A MIRACLE

Nicodemus sits himself down and launches in.

> 'Rabbi, we know you are a teacher who has come from God. For no-one could perform the miraculous signs you are doing if God were not with him.' (3:2)

'From my reading of the Old Testament', he is saying, 'I know the signs to look for. Are you who I think you are? And if you are, what can you tell me about how to get into the kingdom?'

Jesus looks Nicodemus in the eye and declares, 'I tell you the truth, no-one can see the kingdom of God unless he is born again' (3:3). Jesus is saying, 'Nicodemus, if you want to

get into the kingdom of God you need to be born again.'
What puts us at a slight disadvantage here is that as far as we
are concerned, 'born again' means 'fanatic'. We don't mind
rugby fanatics or Rachmaninov fanatics, but we worry about
religious fanatics. We have seen them outside Parliament
waving their placards. We have been cornered by them at
parties. They stand too close and give you more eye contact
than you are really looking for. You do everything you can to
change the subject, but they will not budge. We can't help
feeling that they are slightly unhinged. You need to know that
Jesus is not telling Nicodemus to become a fanatic. What he
is telling Nicodemus could not be more stone-cold sobering.

A few years ago my wife took me to see a ballet. I had
never seen a ballet before, and I have to confess that I found
it hard to muster up much enthusiasm. For some reason I
assumed that I would find it immensely irritating. But five
minutes into *Swan Lake*, I was mesmerized. It had never
occurred to me that watching music unfold through dance
could be so compelling.

What if I had been so smitten by the whole experience
that I had said, 'Right, that's it! I am going to pack it all in
and become a ballet dancer'? I show up at the Royal Ballet
School for an audition. I dance my piece. A few days later a
letter arrives.

Dear Mr Cain,
We regret to inform you that we are unable to offer a place at the
Royal Ballet School. We feel that it is only fair to advise you at
this stage that it is our considered opinion that your only hope of
a career as a ballet dancer would be for you to be born again.

What are they saying to me? They are not saying, 'Mr Cain, if you become a fanatic and practise night and day on your pirouettes and your demi-pliés, then we will give you a place.' What they are saying is, 'Mr Cain, you are too old and too fat and you have two left feet. As you are, you haven't a chance of making it as a ballet dancer. You have not got the ability, nor even the potential. If you want to be a ballet dancer, your only hope is to be born again – only this time as somebody possessed of a little coordination. What you need, Mr Cain, is a miracle.'

Jesus is saying, 'When it comes to getting into the kingdom of God, what you need, Nicodemus, is a miracle.'

And we're thinking, 'Hold on. Doesn't Jesus know who Nicodemus is?'

Jesus knows exactly who he is. And what he says to him explodes everything we have ever been brought up to think about religion.

What we have been brought up to think is that, *if* there is a God, then he'll go for the good guys. He will draw a line, and everyone above it will be let into his kingdom and everyone below it shut out. And we're not saying we are perfect, but, as we open up the newspaper and read of genocide and rape and robbery, we reckon we are definitely better than some people we could mention. If there are people below the line, then they're not people like us. So if there is a God, people like us will squeeze into his kingdom. We reckon.

But Nicodemus was a very good guy. You could not find anyone better than Nicodemus. If you had met him, not only would you have been impressed by him, but you would probably have liked him. He was honest and sincere. He took his religion and other people seriously. If Nicodemus doesn't qualify for a place in the kingdom of God, what hope is there for any of us?

THE KINGDOM OF GOD IS BETTER THAN WE IMAGINE

Part of the reason we assume we'll squeeze in is that we haven't got our heads round what the kingdom of God is like. It is not a club for the reasonably respectable. It is a world made new. There will be no fighting, no fear, no farewells and no funerals. There'll be no broken homes and no broken hearts. We won't need hospitals and we won't even need house-keys, because everything will be the way the King wants it to be. And, best of all, the people will be the way the King wants them to be.

It may be that you worry that it sounds as though we are all going to have to be on our best behaviour. And from our memories of family trips to visit great-aunts, we all know how stifling that can be. But what we need to understand is this: in the kingdom of God people will be good. I don't mean *horribly* good. I mean genuinely good. It will be a pleasure to be with them. What will make it a pleasure is that they will be not so much people who are good at keeping rules as people who are good at relationships. The way they will treat one another will reflect God's ways. Think of what we saw of God in the last chapter. Imagine a world where everyone is as gracious and as true to their word as God is.

This is why Nicodemus looked forward to it so much. But this is also why, when it comes to getting into the kingdom of God, you and I and Nicodemus have a problem. God cannot let me into his kingdom because – as I am – I would spoil it. It is going to be a place of no tears – but I make people cry. It is a place of harmony – but I fall out with people. It is place of truth – but I lie. And I suspect that you do, too.

The question is: why are we like this? Why do rumours of promotion cause such tension in your office? Why do you get nervous on your way to a dinner party with people you don't know very well? Why do family celebrations so often collapse into family rows? It is because we are all playing the same game. The Bible says we are all playing at being god.

KINGS IN CONFLICT

In our culture, we are smitten by the idea that each of us is a 'gifted world maker'. And so we celebrate the fact that there is no one authoritative account of the world by becoming the authors of our own worlds. We tell the story as each of us sees it. In the story of our lives we determine what is true and what is right and what things mean. We live as we see fit to live. The whole enterprise sounds so fertile. But it has led us out of the garden, up the path and into a wasteland.

What happens when the stories collide? What if in your story *you* get the promotion and in mine *I* do? What if in your story *you* get the place on the team and in my story *I* do? What if in your story this land belongs to your people and in mine it is ours? What if in your story your people want to wipe my people off the face of the planet? What happens if in my story what I am doing is morally right and in your story what I am doing is morally wrong?

God is the King of the universe. He created it all and is working out his good plan for it all. But, rather than all of us uniting in his good will for his great kingdom, each of us plays king. We hatch our own little plans for our own little kingdoms. But when your plan and my plan clash, whose plan do we go with? If you are king and I am king, when we meet, who gets to sit on the throne? So we fight for it. That is why the story of humankind is a story of war. Not just with bombs over Basra, but with words over the washing-up. Each of us is fighting to get our own way.

Philosophers talk about how we use language as an instrument of power. They suggest that with our words we don't just describe reality, we create it. If you say something loud enough – or say it with a gun to someone's head, or with control over the media – you can impose your reality on someone else. It turns out that this is just a fancy way of talking about what the Bible calls 'sin'.

Sin is not what we think it is. It is not about going wrong on a few of God's rules, but about going wrong in our whole relationship with God. You see, sin is when we set ourselves up as God, so that instead of living for his will, each of us is living for our own will. And the result is a world in conflict. Each of us has been wounded in the crossfire. But the fact is that each of us has fired our share of the bullets, too. In our world we are at war with one another because we are at war with God.

The reason why the kingdom of God will be a place of peace is because it will be full of people who treat God as God. They will recognize him as the one true King and they will delight to live for his good will.

And that is not me. And it is not you.

REBELS AGAINST THE KING

When it comes to the kingdom of God, you and I are rebels. We may not think of ourselves as rebels. But that is what we are.

When I was seven years old, my favourite TV programme was a show called *The Six-Million-Dollar Man*. It was about an astronaut who'd been in a high-speed crash and had had parts of his body rebuilt (at a cost of six million dollars), so that he could do superhuman things. He would regularly outrun cars, uproot trees and read top-secret documents at a distance of several miles. The show ran from 6.30pm until 7.30pm, and bedtime was at 7pm. At 7pm Mum would come in and say, 'Boys, bedtime.' And what do you think my brother and I would do? We would do absolutely nothing. We just carried on watching the TV as though she wasn't there. We didn't go round denying her existence or beating her up with a cricket bat. But just by sitting there watching TV, we were rebelling.

God says to us all, 'I made you for myself. Will you have me as your God? Will you love me with all your heart and mind and soul and strength? Will you live for me?' And what do we do? Absolutely nothing. We might not go round blowing up churches or distributing pamphlets that deny the existence of God. We just act as though he wasn't there.

Most people I speak to about this feel torn. At the deepest level they know that he is there, calling to them. But there is another level on which they don't want to face up to the fact that he is there. It is not so much that they have a whole raft of intellectual objections, more that they just want to be allowed to stay up late and watch *The Six-Million-Dollar Man*, as it were. They don't want anyone telling them what to do. In their world, they want to be in charge. It is a curious thing that, although we don't want to treat God as King, by a sleight of thought we presume that we are the sort of people who will all be part of his kingdom in the end – even though his kingdom is the place where everyone treats God as King.

It might be that you resent the idea that you are a rebel.

Our only hope of life is to be restored to the relationship with God that we were created for.

Perhaps you feel that 90% of the way you run your life is in line with God's ways and that you would be just the sort of person to fit into his kingdom perfectly. But it's the remaining 10% that gives the game away. What you are saying is, 'God, 90% of what you say is pretty good, I'll go along with that. But 10% is unrealistic, out of date and out to spoil my fun.'

If that is what you are saying to God, who is on the throne of your life? You are. Ninety per cent of God's ways happen to line up with how you think, but on the 10% over which you and God disagree you reserve the right to determine how you want to live. The 10% reveals that, although you may be a good person, you don't treat God as your King.

Some of the whales on the beach may be better than others. For all we know, some of them may even do a lot of work for charity. But that won't bring them life. Their only hope of life is to be restored to the ocean. Jesus wants us to know that being decent people, like Nicodemus, will not bring us life. Our only hope of life is to be restored to the relationship with God that we were created for, to live with God as our King.

TRAPPED IN OUR REBELLION

'All right,' you say. 'Let's imagine, for a moment, that this is all true. Here is Nicodemus and he wants to be part of the kingdom of God. For that matter, here am I and I want to be part of the kingdom of God. Why all this talk of being born again? Why can't I just change my ways and start treating God as King?'

Here is the shattering thing that Jesus is saying. He is saying, 'You *can't* change your ways.'

It is not just that we *don't* treat God as King. It is that we *can't*. We have been born and bred into a world that has walked out on God. Putting ourselves at the centre of things is in our blood. It's the culture we have been steeped in. It has been well said that 'the heart of the human problem is the problem of the human heart'. Our hearts are like a bowling ball with a bias in it that makes it veer off in one particular direction. I can polish myself up on the outside as much as I like, but what I am like on the inside means that again and again I veer off in a selfish direction. That is why there is no place for me in the kingdom of God. The kingdom of God is like a foreign country. They do things differently there. As things stand, I won't fit in. My only hope is a miracle.

Nicodemus is outraged.

'How can a man be born when he is old?' Nicodemus asked. 'Surely he cannot enter a second time into his mother's womb to be born!' (3:4)

'What am I supposed to do? Get back inside my mother's womb, hope I turn out differently this time? I haven't come to be insulted by this primitive talk of miracles and sin. I came for some enlightened conversation about the kingdom of God!'

Jesus has hit Nicodemus' button. And it could be that he has hit yours too. He is saying one of the things that our culture doesn't want to hear. But it seems to me that what he is saying makes sense of how things really are in our world. We long to be better children, better friends or better parents, but there is a gap between the people we long to be and the people we actually are. We wish we weren't so bitter, but we can't seem to move on. We say things we wish we hadn't said. We do things we regret. We keep hurting the people we most love. We vow that we will never do it again, but we just can't seem to kick the habit. Our tongues seem to be beyond our control. Our tempers seem to keep getting the better of us. Our intentions to tidy up just seem to melt when the football comes on. And what is it we say to the people whose hearts we break? 'I didn't mean to fall in love with him. It just happened. I promise you, I never meant to hurt you.' Jesus is not saying that we are all monsters. He is saying that we are all trapped in our rebellion. Like the whale on the beach, we are not free to be the people we were created to be.

I wish I was better at identifying trees, but mostly I need to get up close and look at the fruit to be sure. If there are cherries, then that is the clue that I need to be sure that I am looking at a cherry tree. Like fruit on the branches, our words and deeds show us the kind of tree that we really are. It strikes me that the evidence lines up with what Jesus is saying. Look at my words and deeds, and they show you that in my heart I put myself first. Jesus is saying that I can make any number of resolutions and fill my evenings with all manner of self-help courses, but, like the whale on the beach, the only solution to my problem is to get back into the ocean. If I am going to change, then I need the longings of my heart to change. I need to love God more than I love myself. But just as the whale cannot get itself back into the ocean, all the evidence points to the fact that I cannot change my heart. We need someone to intervene. And that is exactly what Jesus says he has come to do.

THE MIRACLE OF A NEW HEART

In my job as a vicar, I regularly meet people who tell me, with sadness, that they have tried Christianity and found that it doesn't work. They say that it didn't seem to make any difference to their lives and God still seemed as distant as ever. They say they have gone to church and have tried to be better people and have even got involved in some sort of charity work. And I have to break it to them that what they tried was not Christianity.

Jesus did not come to help us to turn over a new leaf. He came to give us a new life. Listen to what he says.

Jesus answered, 'I tell you the truth, no-one can enter the kingdom of God unless he is born of water and the Spirit. Flesh gives birth to flesh, but the Spirit gives birth to spirit. You should not be surprised at my saying, "You must be born again." The wind blows wherever it pleases. You hear its sound, but you cannot tell where it comes from or where it is going. So it is with everyone born of the Spirit.'

'How can this be?' Nicodemus asked.

'You are Israel's teacher,' said Jesus, 'and do you not understand these things?' (3:5–10)

Nicodemus doesn't seem to follow. But in verse 10 Jesus insists that, as Nicodemus is a professor of theology, he should know his Old Testament. This talk of 'new birth' is not new-fangled. It is no more than what the prophets promised. Way back, God had said, through the prophet Ezekiel:

I will sprinkle clean water on you, and you will be clean ... I will give you a new heart ... I will put my Spirit in you. (Ezekiel 36:25–27)

God had promised that one day he would come and do a miracle in the lives of his people. He would give us the new heart that we need, so we can make the new start that we long for. It would be so radical that it would be like a new birth.

I have two children. In the womb Tom and Esther had eyes, but they couldn't see me. They had ears, but they didn't recognize my voice. In the womb they didn't know me. But once they were born into our world, everything changed. They opened their eyes to see me pulling goofy faces at them. They could begin to identify the strange noise that they heard as my voice, singing to them. Their birth marked the beginning of our relationship.

Before God does the miracle of new birth in us, we have eyes, but not for him. We have ears, but they are closed to his voice. We are at best dimly aware of him. And to people like that Jesus does not say, 'You must go to church more, and try harder to be better people.' He says, 'You must be born again.' A Christian is not someone who is gritting their teeth and trying to keep God's rules, but someone who has been born into a living relationship with God. The new birth means that our eyes are opened to see what he is really like. And when we see how good he is, we begin to love him, so that instead of blocking our ears to his voice, we delight to open up the Bible and listen to how he wants his people to live. He has changed our hearts, which means he has changed our deepest longings. We used to live to please ourselves, but now we have thrown away our paper crowns and we live to please our King.

And living with God as our King is not drudgery. Like whales that have been restored to the ocean, new birth has restored us to the life we were created for. So it is when we start to live for God and reflect his ways that we are set free to love other people in the way that we have longed to love them.

Please don't mis-hear this. Christians are not claiming to be perfect. We are not robots that God re-programs at the flick of a switch one Wednesday afternoon. We are people who are feeling their way into a new relationship. Each day we learn more of what God loves and what he hates, and so we learn more of what it means to live for him. But there is also plenty to *un*learn. The old patterns of behaving are deeply ingrained. But the difference is that, now we are restored to the ocean, God has given us the power to begin to change that we never had when we were lying helpless on the beach.

I think of a woman who had become very bitter and angry. When she became a Christian, one of the first things she did was to get in touch with her ex-husband and forgive him for all that he had done to her. I think of a man whom people thought of as insufferably abrasive and arrogant. God has put his Spirit into this man's heart and is changing him into one of the humblest and gentlest people I know. I think of a father who didn't seem to want to engage with his children, but in whom God is now at work, helping him to open up. These are people who have been set free to change because, by his Spirit, God has changed their hearts. Instead of living for themselves, they have been restored to living for him.

Jesus says that there is a sense in which this new life is like the wind.

The wind blows wherever it pleases. You hear its sound, but you cannot tell where it comes from or where it is going. So it is with everyone born of the Spirit. (3:8)

We can tell when the wind is blowing – leaves rustle, hats blow off, shutters slam – but we can't make it windy. You can tell when God has given new life to people – you can see it in the transformation in their lives. But we can't engineer this new birth for ourselves. There is nothing you can do to make the wind blow. You do not get into the kingdom of God because you are better than anyone else. You get in because God has done a miracle in you.

This is really important. For as long as you think you will get into the kingdom of God by trying harder to be better than other people, you will, as Jesus said to Nicodemus, 'never see the kingdom of God'. The only people in whom God does the miracle of new birth are those who acknowledge that, when it comes to getting into the kingdom of God, they are completely helpless.

JESUS IS OUR ONLY HOPE OF LIFE

To make his point, Jesus reminds Nicodemus of something that happened to the Israelites in the desert at the time of Moses, centuries and centuries ago.

The Israelites had been moaning and whinging and making out that they didn't need God. So, in order to remind them just how much they needed him, God sent poisonous snakes into the camp. Once anyone was bitten, they got sick and were sure to die. In desperation, the people cried out for Moses to do something. God told Moses to make a bronze snake and put it up on to a pole, and that any Israelite who looked towards the snake would be healed. Looking to the snake meant acknowledging just how desperately you needed God. You were dying, there was nothing you could do to save yourself, and your only hope of life lay in the snake that God had provided.

It is a strange story. The key is not to be sidetracked into wondering about the mechanics of the whole operation, but to notice the pattern. The people were dying, there was nothing they could do, and their only hope of life was to look to the snake on the pole. Jesus says that this is a pattern that points to him.

> Just as Moses lifted up the snake in the desert, so the Son of Man must be lifted up, that everyone who believes in him may have eternal life. (3:14–15)

Like the snake on the pole, Jesus is going to be lifted up on a cross. Like the people of Israel, we are dying. Our sin has fatally wounded us. And our only hope of life is to look to the cross. The life that he promises to those who look to the cross is 'eternal life'. 'Eternal life' is not something that kicks in when we die, but a relationship with God that starts now and lasts for ever.

In a later chapter we will look at *how*, on the cross, Jesus draws death's sting from us. But for now, Nicodemus has come to Jesus to ask how he can enter the kingdom of God. Jesus' answer is this: 'Nicodemus, the way to enter the kingdom of God is to recognize that you are dying and that there is nothing you can do to save yourself. Look to my death as your only hope. And as you put your trust in me, God will do a miracle in you. Because of my death, you will live. Now and for ever.'

On the whole, our pride means we would prefer it if Jesus had said, 'In order to get into the kingdom of God you need to try harder to be better people. Here are the rules to keep, the rituals to perform. Here is the course you've got to go on; here is the journey you need to make.' We like that. It is a lot more affirming than 'you need a miracle', because it makes us feel that our eternal destiny is something that we can work out for ourselves. But what does it say about God? When Jesus tells us about our helplessness, there is a sense in which it knocks us down. But when you see what it reveals about God's love for us, nothing could be more uplifting. The God of the Bible doesn't just sit back and watch us floundering on the beach, trying to work our way back into the ocean. He doesn't leave us dying. Because he loves us, he takes action. He comes to give us life.

What Jesus says next sums up his whole message to us:

'For God so loved the world that he gave his one and only Son, that whoever believes in him shall not perish but have eternal life.' (3:16)

When we first read that 'God so loved the world', we think that loving the world is just part of his job description. So we wonder what all the fuss is about. But in John's Gospel the word 'world' is used in an almost technical sense. It refers not so much to our planet as to our culture. It is shorthand for a way of living that refuses to treat God as God. Jesus is saying God so loved the 'people-who-walked-out-on-him-and-despised-him-and-thought-he-was-a-joke-so-they-used-his-name-as-a-swear-word' that 'he gave his one and only Son'.

We like to think that everything is OK with us, and assume that this means that God's OK with us. Which makes the whole subject of God one that we don't feel in any sort of a hurry to get round to. Jesus says things are not OK. His message has an urgent claim on our lives, because the situation is worse than we thought. We have rebelled against our King. There is a danger of perishing. If he had left us stranded on the beach, we would have understood. That is how we treat those who have hurt us. But, in his love, the Father asked the Son to go to die for us. And in his love the Son said 'Yes', knowing what it would cost him. Knowing that it would mean being lifted up on a cross to die.

There is nothing we want more than to be loved. Did you know that you were loved like this? If you were to discover that you were loved by the most beautiful, funniest and kindest girl (boy) you'd ever met, I take it that that would not be a matter for indifference. You would want to find out more. John is saying you are loved by the God of the universe. This is not a matter for indifference.

Don't walk away from a love like this.

Don't walk away from a love like this.

Nicodemus came in the dark. We don't know how long he stayed, but from what we read further on in John's Gospel (see 19:39), he left in the light. He came to Jesus as a dead man. He went home with a new heart.

✤ ✤ ✤

We've seen *how* we start a relationship with God, but you might be wondering *who* can start a relationship with God.

Chapter 5

THE LOVE THAT WE LONG FOR
John 4:1–18

It had been a hard morning's walk. Jesus and his disciples were making the three-day trek from Judea up north to Galilee. When they reached a town in Samaria called Sychar, they took a break. The disciples all headed off to find somewhere that would sell them some sandwiches and a cup of coffee. And John says:

> Jesus, tired as he was from the journey, sat down by the well. It was about the sixth hour. When a Samaritan woman came to draw water, Jesus said to her, 'Will you give me a drink?' (His disciples had gone into the town to buy food.) (4:6–8)

While Jesus was waiting for the others to come back, a woman approached with a jar to draw water from the well.

The 'sixth hour' was noon. Nobody went out to draw water in the heat of the midday sun. The women would normally come out together in the cool of the day. But this woman came at noon. And she came alone. Further on in the story we find out why. She had had five husbands and was currently living with another man. We don't know the details. Perhaps she was a serial adulteress and one husband after the other had found grounds to divorce her. Perhaps her first husband had died and she had been bounced into a second marriage too soon. Perhaps her new husband was unable to cope with her grief and so deserted her, and she found herself thrust into a desperate cycle, lurching from one ill-founded relationship to the next. Perhaps she knew that her current set-up had no real future, but she needed a roof over her head and here was someone who was prepared to take her in. We don't know. But the 'good' women of Sychar did not approve. So they froze her out.

The woman lowered her jar and Jesus asked her for a drink. She was caught off guard.

> The Samaritan woman said to him, 'You are a Jew and I am a Samaritan woman. How can you ask me for a drink?' (For Jews do not associate with Samaritans.) (4:9)

In that culture men did not speak to women in public. And *Jewish* men certainly did not speak to *Samaritan* women. John reminds his readers that the Jews (who lived in the south) viewed the Samaritans (who lived in the north) as racially and religiously impure. There was a deep-rooted hostility that went back a very long way. It is not just that Jesus spoke to a woman whom everyone else had shunned, he spoke to a Samaritan woman. In Jesus' day, one of the ways you expressed your disapproval of someone was to refuse to eat or drink with them.

But here is Jesus asking to drink from this woman's cup.

WHOEVER YOU ARE, WHATEVER YOU HAVE DONE, JESUS HAS COME FOR YOU

We've all been made to feel unwelcome. Our path to being accepted has been barred by our colour or our gender or our accent or because we are not as beautiful or as funny or as clever or as cool as the others. And that leaves us feeling not just lonely, but worthless. But there is nothing that leaves us feeling as lonely as when people use our failings as a stick to beat us away with. Your father won't speak to you because of your drugs conviction. Your girlfriend won't see you again because you cheated on her. Your friends melt away when they find out that you have been stealing from the company you work for. You just want a chance to explain. But they have closed the door on you. And on your side of the door it feels very lonely.

When they travelled, all the other religious leaders at the time of Jesus would have avoided going through Samaria. But John says that Jesus 'had to go through Samaria'. He *had* to go because he wanted this woman to know that he was not like all the others. The women of Sychar may have looked down on her, but in his eyes she was precious.

In the last chapter, we saw *how* to get into the kingdom of God. In this chapter we will see *who* gets into the kingdom of God. In the social currency of the day, Nicodemus would have been worth more than this woman. He was a man at the centre of the social whirl. Everyone thought of him as being 'in'. But she was a woman on the edge. Everyone thought of her as being 'out'. In many ways they were opposites. But Jesus looks upon them both with the same love. Whether you are a Nicodemus or a Samaritan woman, it makes no difference to Jesus. His love tears down all the barriers that leave us left out and lonely. It may be that you think that there is no way he could open the door to you. Not after what you have done. In which case, you need to know that Jesus is not gathering a club for a certain type of person. Whoever you are, whatever your story, he has come for you.

JESUS HAS COME TO GIVE US WHAT WE ARE LOOKING FOR

Often, the experience of church we have had has left us with the distinct impression that Jesus is just like everyone else, and that he has come for us because he wants something from us. There are some (like Nicodemus) who assume that they will get into the kingdom of God because they feel that they have a great deal to offer Jesus. There are others (like the Samaritan woman) who assume that they cannot be part of the kingdom of God because they feel that they have nothing to offer Jesus. But here is the reason why Nicodemus and the Samaritan woman stand on level ground. Getting into the kingdom of God is not about what we can give to him. Jesus has come because there is something he wants to give to us.

Jesus answered her, 'If you knew the gift of God and who it is that asks you for a drink, you would have asked him and he would have given you living water.' (4:10)

Jesus is saying: 'Here I am asking you for a drink, but if you knew what I had to give you, you would be asking me, because what I have to give you is living water.' You could take 'living water' to mean 'running water', so she is a bit taken aback.

'Sir,' the woman said, 'you have nothing to draw with and the well is deep. Where can you get this living water? Are you greater than our father Jacob, who gave us the well and drank from it himself, as did also his sons and his flocks and herds?' (4:11–12)

'Look, sunshine,' she says, 'There is no running water round here. If you want water, this is all there is. Jacob, our ancestor, dug this well, and my people have been drawing water from it for generations. Or is our Samaritan water not good enough for your Jewish lips?'
Jesus is undeterred.

Jesus answered, 'Everyone who drinks this water will be thirsty again, but whoever drinks the water I give him will never thirst. Indeed, the water I give him will become in him a spring of water welling up to eternal life.' (4:13–14)

The woman doesn't quite get what Jesus is saying, but her words are a window on her heart.

The woman said to him, 'Sir, give me this water so that I won't get thirsty and have to keep coming here to draw water.' (4:15)

'Never thirst again?' she asks. 'I don't know what sort of water you're talking about. But I could do with some of it. Every day I come here with my empty jar and fill it up. By the next day it's empty again. So back I come for more. That jar is the story of my life.

We too are looking for something that will quench our thirst.

I keep trying to fill it up. But it's not long before it is empty again. And I've got to go and find some way of filling it up. Sir, if you've got water that'll quench my thirst, I could do with some of that.'

This is a woman who is empty on the inside, a woman who is a lot like us, because, like her, we too are looking for something that will quench our thirst.

The search for satisfaction

We tell ourselves that our thirst will be quenched when we get the A-levels we need to get into university. When we get to university, we tell ourselves that if we just get into a band, or onto a team, or get a first, *then* we will be satisfied. That fills us up for a while, but we soon start to feel empty again and tell ourselves that it will be a job and settling down that will really satisfy us. But it's not long before the holidays that our colleagues go on and the lifestyle sections of the weekend papers all conspire to make us feel that we are missing out. If only we had just a little bit more money, then we could buy ourselves the sort of life that really *would* be satisfying. We say. So we work longer hours and climb up the career ladder. But, not long after we can afford to eat in the sort of restaurants that we have always dreamed of eating in, life begins to lose its taste. What would spice things up again would be a trip round the world, we say. We had thought that moving to a bigger house would fill us up. And the fact that it doesn't just makes us feel all the more empty and all the more desperate in our search for something that will. And so we pack our bags and wander round Venice and climb Kilimanjaro and swim with dolphins in Mexico and shoot the rapids in New Zealand. When we come home, we decide that the way forward is to downsize and move to the country, because what would make us really happy would be to have more time in our lives for the things we enjoy. So we retrain, and in our early forties we take up mountain biking and run marathons and learn to play the saxophone and think about emigrating to Australia, because, we say, that is the one thing that really would quench our thirst.

But in our hearts we know it is not true, because we know that it is not some*thing* that we are thirsty for, but some*one*. More than we want a fast car, we want someone to go for a drive with. More than we want a beautiful house, we want someone to make a home with. Even our desire for designer clothes is less about the fact that we love the fabric and more about the fact that we want someone to love us. Our restless

desire for *things* is just one of the ways we distract ourselves
from our real longing for a relationship that will quench our
thirst. We are looking for someone who will make us feel as
if we matter, someone who will give us our reason for being
on this planet.

Like us, the woman at the well was thirsty for someone
to love. But, like us, she had known what it is to be
disappointed in love. There is nothing that can fill us up
like love, nothing that can leave us so empty.

When somebody says to us, 'I love you because you are
beautiful and kind and funny', in theory it is music to our
ears. But in practice it is easily transposed into: 'Today you
are lovely, so I love you. But tomorrow, if you lose your
figure, or if your hair falls out, or if your money runs out, or
if you don't make me laugh any more and I meet someone
who does, then I'm not sure that I will love you any more.'
We call it love, but in fact we have turned people into
tools that we use to fill our emptiness. And if you put two
empty people together in one relationship and each is
looking to be filled by the other, there is always going to be
disappointment.

Amy says that Jake doesn't make her feel loved any more.
They have drifted into the rut of a domestic routine that falls
way short of what Amy had dreamt of. Jake is very busy at
work and seems preoccupied and listless at the weekends,
more passionate about the football than about Amy. He says
he is content with how things are. But he never asks Amy
how she is. When they are together she feels desperately
alone. Jake no longer fills her emptiness. And it is not long
before she leaves him. Like the woman at the well, she picks

up her life like an empty jar and carries it out in search of someone who will fill it up again.

This pattern of filling and emptying, of coming together and then moving on, hurts. It means we have grown more and more afraid to be ourselves. Play the wrong card and the other person may move on. So in our relationships we trace the same pattern that we see in the world around us. Of course they can be so beautiful, and yet they too are shot through with sadness.

Into this woman's sadness Jesus says, 'Go, call your husband and come back' (4:16). That is not a road she wants to go down. She tries to divert him by saying, 'I have no husband' (4:17). But Jesus sees straight through her.

> Jesus said to her, 'You are right when you say you have no husband. The fact is, you have had five husbands, and the man you now have is not your husband. What you have just said is quite true.' (4:17–18)

What is Jesus doing? It looks as if he is being cruel: she admits her emptiness and he then dredges up her past and bangs it like a drum to show her just how empty she is. But he is not like the others. He is not about to close another door on her. He wants to help her to face up to the truth about what she needs. What she really needs.

The story that she tells herself is that she has been unlucky in love. She believes that Mr Right is still out there somewhere, waiting for her, and one day she will find him. Jesus loves her enough to prick her bubble. The fact that all her relationships have ended in disappointment is not just bad luck. It is what happens when we try to live our lives without God. The reason we long for relationships is that we are made in the image of the God of relationship. But until we get our relationship with him right, our relationships with one another will keep going wrong.

One of the reasons they go wrong is because we ask more of other human beings than they are capable of giving us. When we sit the elephant of our expectations on the three-legged stool of the person we love, it is no surprise that something gives way. If I ask another person to be the reason that I am on this planet, I am asking them to be for me what only God can be. If I ask another person to fill up my emptiness, I am asking them to do for me what only God can do. That is why Jesus wants us to know that the longing that we have for a relationship that will make sense of our lives is a longing for a relationship with the God who made us. Our deepest thirst can be quenched only by the water that he gives.

The water that quenches our deepest thirst

We need water to live. Go without it, and we wither and die. The Bible describes God as 'the spring of living water' (Jeremiah 17:13). We need him to live. Go without him, and we wither and die on the inside.

The promises of the Old Testament are made to parched people like us. Through the prophet Isaiah God promises that, by his Spirit, he will come into our lives, like water pouring down onto a bone-dry land. And like flowers unfurling in the rain, our souls will be revived (Isaiah 44:3–4).

And Jesus is saying that God has kept his promise. Jesus has come to give us the water we so desperately thirst for. It is the water that wells up 'to eternal life'. We've seen that 'eternal life' is about a relationship with God. Jesus wants us to know that if we drink of this relationship, we will never thirst again.

I remember when it first struck me that Jesus was saying just the opposite of what I was expecting. I was cornered into following Jesus by the truth of his claims – there seemed to be no mistaking the direction in which the signs were pointing. But there were times when I tagged along half-heartedly, fearing that following him was a bit like going on a diet. Forsaking the steak and ale pie of life, I would have to endure a cabbage-soup kind of existence. But I had confused Jesus with the poet William Blake's 'priests in black gowns' who were 'walking their rounds' and 'binding with briars my joys and desires'.[1] Did you notice the direction in which Jesus' conversation with this woman is heading? He is not telling her that her problem is that her appetite for life is too large and he has come to curb her desires. What he is saying is that her desires are too small, and he has come to enlarge them. In one of his addresses C. S. Lewis puts it well:

> We are half-hearted creatures, fooling about with drink and sex and ambition, when infinite joy is offered us. Like an ignorant child who wants to go on making mud pies in a slum because he can't understand what's meant by the offer of a holiday at the sea. We are far too easily pleased.[2]

Our problem is not that we run after too much pleasure, but that we run after pleasures that are too small. We have tried to satisfy our thirst in muddy wells of our own making. Jesus has come to bring streams of pure running water.

It is true that when Jesus calls us to follow him, there are lies and lusts that he calls us to turn from. But that is not because he wants to stop us being happy. It is because he created us and knows better than we do that the things we run after don't actually make us happy. He knows that true happiness is found only in knowing the God who made us. *He* is the one who gives us our reason for being on this planet. *He* is the one who fills our emptiness.

The journalist and broadcaster Malcolm Muggeridge wrote these words:

> I may, I suppose, regard myself, or pass for being, a relatively successful man. People occasionally stare at me in the streets – that's fame. I can fairly easily earn enough to qualify for admission to the higher slopes of the Inland Revenue – that's success. Furnished with money and a little fame even the elderly, if they care to, may partake of trendy diversions – that's pleasure. It might happen once in a while that something I said or wrote was sufficiently heeded for me to persuade myself that it represented a serious impact on our time – that's fulfilment. Yet I say to you, and I beg you to believe me, multiply these tiny triumphs by a million, add them all together, and they are nothing – less than nothing, a positive impediment – measured against one draught of that living water Christ offers to the spiritually thirsty, irrespective of who or what they are.[3]

My grandmother is a remarkable woman. She has not had five husbands, but she has had four. And she has known some of the pain and disappointment that the woman at the well must have known. When she first drank of the water that Christ has come to give us she was in her seventies, and she wrote me a letter. Her name is Joy. She wrote, 'All my life I have been looking for Joy. And now in Jesus I have found the happiness that I longed for. I have found Joy.' In God we find the love that we have been longing for.

It may be that you are beginning to feel that all this talk of Jesus and love is a little sickly-sweet. You fear that this book is taking a nose-dive into the sort of romantic comedy that you normally try to avoid. But it is not just the love of a lover that we have longed for. Think of the father whose love you have tried so hard to win. No matter how well you do in your exams, it never seems to be good enough to please him. You wish that – just once – he would tell you how much you mean to him.

In God we find the love that we have been longing for.

Think of the older brother who always seems so embarrassed by the fact that you are not as cool as he is. And you wish he would be even just a little bit proud of you. Think of the friend you had wanted to go travelling with, but who made his own plans and didn't even think to include you.

Here is the love you long for.

You can see it in the way that Jesus treats this woman. Everyone else has written her off. But God is not like everyone else. He is not saying that if we polish up our act and keep our nose clean and start going to church and giving

to charity, then maybe he might think about loving us. She
has done nothing to deserve God's love. In fact, like the rest
of us, she has walked out on God. And yet he still loves her.
You see, he doesn't do love like everyone else does love. He
doesn't love us because we make the grade, which means
he doesn't stop loving us when we mess up. He loves us
because that is the sort of God he is. And he is not going to
change. Which means his love for us is not going to change.

A little later on, the woman urges the people of the
town to meet Jesus for themselves by saying, 'Come, see a
man who told me everything I ever did' (4:29). Isn't that
remarkable? Jesus knows the truth about her. And he knows
the truth about us. But the thing is, he doesn't walk away.
Here, at last, is a relationship in which we are free to be
ourselves. We can lay all our cards on the table. We can
be honest about what we are like and what we have done.
And he will not walk away. Ever.

Whoever you are, this is the love that you long for. It will
fill up your emptiness.

The water that revives our relationships

We said that until we get our relationship with God right,
our relationships with one another will keep going wrong.
The flip side of that is that when we do get right with God, it
transforms our relationships with one another.

If I am right with God, I am no longer looking to you to
fill my emptiness, because God has already filled me. And
out of that fullness I can love you as I never loved you before.
So, even on the days when you have very little to give me, on
the days when you are grumpy, or distracted by work, or you

are lying in bed ill, or you don't ask me how I am, or you don't help me with the washing-up -- even on those days, I still have something to give you. Because God has filled up my emptiness.

If you were wondering whether you were the sort of person who could have a relationship with God, Jesus wants you to know that whoever you are, whatever you have done, he has come to give you the relationship with God that you long for. He has come to quench your thirst.

✤   ✤   ✤

If I were reading this, I think I would be thinking: 'Yes, but just because you and this Malcolm Muggeridge bloke find this "living water" satisfying, it doesn't mean that I will. After all, some people find satisfaction in tidying the garden shed.'

In the next chapter we will see that it is not just that whoever you are, whatever your story, Jesus has come for you. Whoever you are, whatever your story, the life that Jesus brings is the satisfaction that you long for.

NOTES

1. William Blake, 'The Garden of Love', from *Songs of Experience*.
2. C. S. Lewis, 'The Weight of Glory' (SPCK, 1942); republished in *The Weight of Glory and Other Addresses* (Zondervan, 2001), p. 26.
3. Quoted in Bruce Milne, *The Message of John* (IVP, 1993), p. 84.

Chapter 6

THE REVOLUTION
John 4:19–42

The reason that the life Jesus brings is satisfying is because he restores us to the reason we are on this planet. He makes it possible for us to worship God.

I realize that this doesn't sound at all promising. I speak to many people whose idea of worshipping God is bound up with having to go along to church. And, frankly, they can think of better things to do with their Sunday mornings than to sit in a draughty old building singing dreary old hymns. Worshipping God sounds as if it will take us further and further away from everything that makes life rich and exciting, and lead us down a religious road that is relentlessly narrow and grey.

But what Jesus wants us to see is that worshipping God is the very thing that opens us up to a richer experience of the world. It means that every corner of our lives matters and every moment is charged with meaning. It is true that worshipping God will mean being part of a community of Christians. But worshipping God is about something much bigger than going along to church. God doesn't just want your Sunday mornings. He wants you.

A COPERNICAN REVOLUTION
Until the sixteenth century most people thought that the sun revolved around the earth. Then Nicolaus Copernicus famously stood up and said that in fact it was just the opposite. The earth revolved around the sun.

Worshipping God will mean a Copernican revolution in our lives. We have laboured under the delusion that we are at the centre of the universe. But God calls us to recognize that he is in fact at the centre of the universe. And so he wants us to make him the reason we get out of bed in the morning.

To that, there is a little bit of us that wants to ask, 'What is his problem?'

If I were to tell everyone who reads this book to make me the reason they get out of bed in the morning, that would be ugly. It is what cult leaders and power-crazed dictators do. It is ugly because it is a distortion of reality. I am not at the centre of the universe, and you were not created to live for me. But God *is* at the centre of the universe and we *were* created to live for him. So when he calls us to worship him, it is not to constrict our lives, but to restore us to the reason we are on this planet by restoring us to the relationship with him that we were made for. The bottom line is that worshipping God is about a relationship with God in which we creatures treat him as our Creator.

As the Creator he cares about every corner of his creation. There are not 'spiritual' and 'non-spiritual' areas of life. He wants us to worship him on the football pitch. Not by singing hymns at half-time, but by treating our team-mates and our opponents with the kind of love that reflects his love. He wants us to make music in a way that celebrates his creativity. He wants us to do all our studies in a way that honours his truth. He wants us to spend our money in a way that reflects his priorities. He wants us to vote in a way that reflects his passion for justice. He wants us to treat people in a way that reflects the way he has treated us. So, whether we are doing the weekly shop, climbing a mountain, driving a car, seeing a client, or watching a movie, he wants us to do it all in a way that pleases him.

It may be that this confirms all your worst fears. This doesn't sound as if it will quench your thirst for life at all. It sounds as though living for this God is going to squeeze you dry. But we all have things in our lives that we would do anything for. Things we couldn't live without. Things that are – in effect – our gods. It seems to me that it is worth pausing and reflecting on what living for your gods does to your life.

IS YOUR GOD BIG ENOUGH?

If you live for your career, what impact does that have on your relationships? Maybe you feel more at home at work than at home. At work, people know who you are. You know who you are. But in social settings you don't really know what to say to anyone. Physically you are at the party, but mentally you are still at the office. When we worship at the altar of our career, it pulls us away from our family and makes us restless at weekends. Time away from work becomes time that we can't make sense of.

Or what if you don't live so much for work as for the weekends? What impact does that have on how you feel about your existence from Monday to Friday? If you worship the god of pleasure, it is no surprise that at work you feel you are just killing time, watching the clock, until you can come to life on a Friday night.

The small gods that we worship set one area of our lives against another, and so tear us apart. But the God who created us comes to put our lives back together again. He is like the conductor of an orchestra. Without the conductor, there is discord: the oboes come in early, the brass section is too loud and the poor violas can't even be heard. In the music of our lives, our relationships want to come in first, but they get drowned out by the exams and you can't even hear the hobbies we used to enjoy. The cellos are in no position to bring in the bassoons. What they need is the conductor. My career is in no position to bring in my family. What I need is the Creator, who stands over every area of my life to bring them all together in harmony. And when he waves his baton, it is not to murder the music we are trying to play, but to bring life.

So, for example, living to please God in the office will mean that we work hard with honesty and integrity, and that we treat our colleagues graciously and fairly. But because the Creator wants us to please him in *every* area of our lives, working in a way that pleases God will also mean knowing

when to *stop* work, in order to go home and spend time with
family and friends. The God who created us wants us to
enjoy the world he created for us. So, at the weekend, when
we have a leisurely meal with friends, or go for a long walk in
the hills, or drift round an art gallery, we are not wasting
time. These are all things we can do to please God, because
they are all part of what it means to worship him. And on a
Monday morning, we don't have to become someone else
who is doing something else unconnected to the fun that we
had at the weekend. At the weekend we were worshipping
God. And on Monday morning we are doing the same.
Living with him at the centre is what harmonizes the
different areas of our lives and gives us a purpose that holds
our lives together.

I read a fascinating conversation in the newspaper,
between two top-class sportsmen who were suffering from
long-term injuries. The rugby player asked the footballer,
'Do you ever get that feeling on a Saturday: "I am a football
player and I am not playing, so what am I?" I am a bit
purposeless.' If we find our meaning in what we do, what
happens when we can no longer do it? Do we just have to
resign ourselves to becoming 'purposeless'? Or is there a
purpose that is bigger than the one that our small gods
give us?

As a Christian I may love music, really enjoy my job and
have a passion for mountain-biking, but none of those
things, in itself, is big enough to be the reason that I am on
this planet. They are good things to enjoy, but they are too
small to worship. If I were a professional rugby player
who worshipped God, then I would find real pleasure in

playing rugby. But my deepest pleasure in life would come from living to please God. Rugby would be just one of the areas in which I was living to please him. So if, one Saturday afternoon, I broke my leg and could never play rugby again, it would be a dark, dark day, but not a day for despair. In the days after my injury my reason for being on this planet would be the same as it was in the days before it. If I am living for the God who created me, then in him I have an unbreakable reason for being on this planet.

Living for God transforms the dark days when everything else seems to have fallen through. And it also transforms the dull days. Worshipping God does not mean that we will be guaranteed an exciting job. But worshipping God at work will transform Mondays to Fridays. It's not that if you worship God then stuffing envelopes will suddenly become satisfying. But if at work you seek to please him in the way you work, and in the way you treat your colleagues, then you will no longer feel that from Mondays to Fridays you are just killing time. The work itself may be unfulfilling, but you will find fulfilment in the fact that you are living for the God who made you.

That is why Jesus describes the life that he brings as 'water'. When your thirst is quenched, your whole body is revived. When your thirst is quenched by God, your whole life is revived. When you worship God, you are not just a whale trying to find ways of occupying yourself on the beach. You are back in the ocean.

If you and I are to get back into the ocean, what will we need?

WHAT WILL WE NEED IN ORDER TO WORSHIP GOD?

Let's go back to the woman at the well.

> 'Sir,' the woman said, 'I can see that you are a prophet. Our fathers worshipped on this mountain, but you Jews claim that the place where we must worship is in Jerusalem.' (4:19–20)

'All right,' says the woman. 'You seem to be some kind of a prophet. You tell me that if I want my thirst quenched I need to start worshipping God. But how do I do it? I am a Samaritan. We worship God our way, here on Mount Gerizim. You're a Jew. Are you asking me to become a Jew, and worship God your way, in the temple in Jerusalem? I mean, which religion are you asking me to sign up for here?'

But Jesus replies, 'Believe me, woman, a time is coming when you will worship the Father neither on this mountain nor in Jerusalem' (4:21). The ancient dispute between these two religions is about to become irrelevant. He says that 'a time is coming and has now come when the true worshippers will worship the Father in spirit and truth, for they are the kind of worshippers the Father seeks' (4:23). This woman won't need to go to a particular *place* in order to worship God. What she will need is 'the Spirit' and 'the truth'.

To worship God we need the Spirit

Jesus explains that 'God is spirit' (4:24). As things stand, we are dead to God. As we saw in chapter 4, it is only by his Spirit that we can be born into a living relationship with him. So Jesus is telling this woman that worshipping God is bigger than she thinks. It is not about going along to certain buildings on a certain day of the week and doffing our hats to a distant God we don't really know. Worshipping God is about a living encounter with him. And if we are going to encounter him we will need more than bricks and mortar. We will need his Spirit in our lives.

To worship God we need the truth

People often tell me that they don't need to go to church to worship God. In one sense that is true. Worshipping God does not depend on going to a particular place. But what people often mean by 'I don't need to go to church to worship God' is something like 'I will find my own way to worship God.' But just as I won't meet with God unless I have his Spirit, I won't know how to treat God unless I know the truth about him. It is the same in all our relationships.

Not long after I met my wife, she told me that she hated oranges. She wanted me to know that it was not just a mild aversion that she was talking about. She hated their texture, their taste and their smell. She does not eat them in any shape or form. Even an orange Smartie is too orangey for her. She simply will not go near an orange – or anyone who has recently eaten an orange. I took the hint. But chocolate, she said, was an altogether different story. Knowing the truth about what my wife hates and what she loves means that I know how to treat her. For her birthday, I do not surprise her with caramelized oranges. It is chocolate cake every time.

If, one year, I bought my wife a bag of oranges for Christmas and said, 'I know you said you hated oranges, but

I love them, and I just can't believe that any sensible person could hate them as much as you say you do', what would you think of me?

When we decide to worship God in our own way, we are doing the spiritual equivalent of buying my wife a bag of oranges. We may think it is a perfectly reasonable thing to do, but it is no way to conduct a relationship. If we are going to have an authentic relationship with God, we will need to know what he hates and what he loves. We will need to know the truth about him.

At this point the woman scratches her head and says, 'I know that Messiah' (called Christ) 'is coming. When he comes, he will explain everything to us' (4:25). She is not sure that she follows all that Jesus is saying, but she knows that the prophets said that when the Messiah came he would bring God's Spirit, and the truth about God would be made known for all to see.

Jesus' answer must have just about taken her breath away: 'I who speak to you am he' (4:26). Jesus is saying that he is the one the prophets were looking forward to. He is the one who will pour out the long-promised Spirit into our hearts, so that we can be born into a living relationship with God. And he is the one who reveals the truth about God in all his brilliance. Jesus brings the Spirit and the truth that we need in order to worship God. And that is why, if we want to worship God, we need to go to Jesus.

To worship God we need to go to Jesus
If this woman had asked her question in Old Testament times, Jesus is clear that the right thing for her to have done

would have been to go to the temple in Jerusalem. He says
'You Samaritans worship what you do not know.' In other
words, the Samaritans (who disregarded most of the Old
Testament) were offering to God the spiritual equivalent of
a bag of oranges. 'We worship what we do know, for
salvation is from the Jews.' Jesus insists that 'salvation is
from the Jews'. So if we want to know how to treat God as
God, we need to look at how he revealed himself to his
people in the Old Testament. By giving them his law, he
made it clear that there is a right and a wrong way to treat
him. By giving them the temple, he made it clear that there
is a right and a wrong place to meet him. The temple was the
upgraded model of the tabernacle. So if you wanted to meet
with God, you had to go to the temple. But, through the
prophets, God insisted that the temple pointed forward to
something bigger. It was, as one New Testament writer puts
it, 'only a shadow of the good things that are coming'
(Hebrews 10:1). Jesus is saying that all that the temple stood
for points forward to him. He is God come to dwell with his
people. So if we want to meet with God, we don't need to go
to a particular building (like a temple or a church), but we *do*
need to go to Jesus.

You need to understand that Jesus is not saying that he is
just *a* way to meet with God that might resonate with some
people. He is making a very startling claim. He is saying,
'Whoever you are, wherever you are from, if you want to
meet with God, come to me.' It's a claim that is rooted in the
Old Testament. The prophets had said that salvation would
flow like a river from the Jews out to all nations – including
Samaritans. And Jesus is saying that that time has come.

After two days with him the Samaritan townspeople concluded 'that this man really is the Saviour of the world' (4:42). They come to exactly the conclusion that John wants all his readers to come to. He wants us to see that through the Jews the one true God has been working out his one true plan of salvation for all people of all nations. And the reason Jesus is the Saviour of the world is because he is the one who has come to bring that plan to its climax.

That is the background to the sort of claim that Jesus will make, a few chapters later in John's Gospel, when he says: 'I am the way and the truth and the life. No-one comes to the Father except through me' (14:6). It is a claim that was as unpopular in the first century as it is in the twenty-first. It is not only that it sounds so arrogant and exclusive. It seems to confirm our suspicions that God is playing hard to get. If he wants everyone to come to know him, then you'd think that he wouldn't much mind how we found our way to him. By narrowing it down to this one way, isn't he making it hard for people to find him?

But imagine that you had been reading this book and you had one or two questions you wanted to run by me, so you got in touch, asking if we could meet for lunch. If I said, 'Fine, I will see you around somewhere. Perhaps we'll bump into each other', how would you feel? You certainly couldn't accuse me of being narrow and exclusive in my plans for meeting. But nor could you accuse me of being terribly keen to meet you. What if I had said, 'Let's meet on Tuesday at 1pm at the Primrose Café on Boyce's Avenue. I will wait for you by the door and you will be able to spot me because I will be wearing a black trilby and a pink carnation in my buttonhole.' That might be a somewhat narrow instruction that would seem to exclude not just other times of the day and days of the week, but other perfectly good cafés in Bristol. But the fact is that, if you took me up on what I said, you and I would definitely be able to meet. Not only would I definitely be there waiting for you, but when you arrived you would certainly be able to recognize me. The 'narrowness' of the instructions is the key to our meeting one another.

I meet a lot of people who tell me that the 'water of life' is not all that it is cracked up to be. But it turns out that they have never tried it. They have tried some form of religion, but it wasn't particularly satisfying. They are not sure if God ever turned up. Jesus is not recommending that this woman take up some form of religion in order to enhance her spiritual well-being – in much the same way that a doctor might tell us to take up some form of exercise in order to enhance our physical well-being. Jesus is making a very particular claim. He is saying that if we turn to *him* we will definitely meet God and our thirst will definitely be quenched. That is because he is not offering us a little bit of religion, in the hope that it might resonate with us. He is the only one who can restore us to the reason we are on this planet, because he is the only one who is able to restore us to the God who made us. Only he can give us the Spirit. Only he can give us the truth. So, whatever sort of a whale we are, whatever sort of a beach we have washed up on, only he can restore us to the ocean.

✣   ✣   ✣

Perhaps you see what Jesus is saying. You see that he is claiming to be the one person who is able to restore us to a worshipping relationship with the God who made us. And you see why, in theory, worshipping God does not narrow down our lives but opens them up. But you have a question that is boiling away within you. You want to know what gives Jesus the right to make such an outrageous claim. Who does he think he is?

Chapter 7

OUR LIFE IN HIS HANDS
John 5:1–30

Some time later, Jesus went up to Jerusalem for a feast of the Jews. Now there is in Jerusalem near the Sheep Gate a pool, which in Aramaic is called Bethesda and which is surrounded by five covered colonnades. Here a great number of disabled people used to lie – the blind, the lame, the paralysed. One who was there had been an invalid for thirty-eight years. (5:1–5)

For thirty-eight years, this paralysed man has watched everyone else walk by. He has seen them hurrying to work, or setting out on a journey with their camels packed impossibly high with provisions. He has watched lovers exchanging glances, strangers asking the way, friends greeting each other across the street and heading off together for a drink. He has smiled at the little children dancing round the pool. For thirty-eight years life has passed him by.

There was a tradition that if an angel came and stirred up the waters, then the first person to climb into the pool would be healed. The man is desperate for a life that he has lost all hope of ever having. So he will try anything. And that's why he is lying by this pool.

> When Jesus saw him lying there and learned that he had been in this condition for a long time, he asked him, 'Do you want to get well?'
> 'Sir,' the invalid replied, 'I have no-one to help me into the pool when the water is stirred. While I am trying to get in, someone else goes down ahead of me.' (5:6–7)

Jesus sees the man, walks up to him and asks if he wants to be healed. The man thinks Jesus is mocking him. 'Do I want to get well? Do ducks quack? Of course I want to get well. Do you think I am here for the conversation? I want to be in that water and away from here as soon as I can. Only I haven't got any mates to carry me in. Instead of asking stupid questions, you could help me. You could hang around with me and wait for this angel to come.' It never occurs to him that Jesus might be extending an invitation: that Jesus was in fact asking him, 'Do you want *me* to make you well?'

> Then Jesus said to him, 'Get up! Pick up your mat and walk.' (5:8)

Jesus just says the word, and the man gets up and does what he has been longing to do for thirty-eight years. He picks up his mat and walks off. Jesus has given him back the life that he longed for.

At once the man was cured; he picked up his mat and walked. (5:9)

The reaction of the religious authorities is stunning:

The day on which this took place was a Sabbath, and so the Jews said to the man who had been healed, 'It is the Sabbath; the law forbids you to carry your mat.' (5:9–10)

The Sabbath was the day of the week that God had set aside as a day of rest for his people. It was a day on which God wanted his people to be free from the burden of work and to enjoy time with him and with family and friends. It was a great blessing to his people. But over the years, the religious authorities had obscured God's original vision for the day behind a wall of rules and regulations about what did and did not constitute work.

So this man has been paralysed for thirty-eight years and he *walks* in carrying his bed over his shoulder, and all they can say is, 'What do you think you are doing, carrying your bed on the Sabbath? Carrying your bed is work. You are not supposed to work on the Sabbath.' The man is healed. This is amazing! But all they can say is, 'You'd better stop this right away.'

Thinking he might get into trouble, the man says, 'Don't blame me. This stranger told me to take up my mat and walk. What was I supposed to do?'

The authorities want to know who it is who has healed
this man on the Sabbath. They want to know who dares to
set himself above their authority. But Jesus has melted away
into the crowd.

Later on, Jesus tracks the man down and says, 'See, you
are well again. Stop sinning or something worse may happen
to you' (5:14). He is not saying that anyone who commits
sin will immediately fall ill or suffer in some way as a direct
consequence of their sin. But sometimes, some of our
suffering does come about as the result of our sin. It might
be our greed that has landed us in debt, or our affair that
broke up the family we loved. It might be that this man
was a bandit who had broken his back during a raid. We
don't know. But Jesus is making it clear that if he goes
back to his old way of life, then something worse than
paralysis will happen to him. And from what Jesus goes on
to say, it is clear that the 'something worse' is God's eternal
judgment.

At this, the man marches straight back to the authorities
and turns Jesus in. And we read, 'So, because Jesus was doing
these things on the Sabbath, the Jews persecuted him'
(5:16). What is it with this man? Why did he hand Jesus
in? You'd think he would have been grateful to Jesus.

It turns out that he is a little bit like us. We don't mind
a Jesus who heals us, or helps us in the thick of our exams.
But we don't want a Jesus who is going to start claiming to
have authority over our lives. Who does he think he is,
telling this man how he should live, threatening him with
God's judgment?

One of John's themes is that Jesus has come into this

world for the sake of people who don't really want him in their lives.

> He came to that which was his own, but his own did not receive him. (1:11)

And that is the theme we see played out by the man and the religious authorities in this scene. Our question is just another variation of theirs. Like the man by the pool and the authorities who want Jesus stopped, we want to know who Jesus thinks he is. What gives him the right to tell us how to live?

We live in a culture that thinks claims such as those Jesus makes are inherently arrogant. But the question to ask is, 'By what authority do they make their claim?' This miracle points to the authority by which Jesus makes his claims.

THE MIRACLE POINTS TO THE FACT THAT JESUS IS EQUAL WITH GOD

When the authorities catch up with Jesus, they want to know what gives him the right to disregard their rules. In reply, rather than draw attention to the way they have twisted God's original intentions for the Sabbath day, Jesus draws attention to himself.

> Jesus said to them, 'My Father is always at his work to this very day, and I, too, am working.' (5:17)

In all their debates about what you could and could not do on the Sabbath, the authorities were agreed that the one person who could continue to work on the Sabbath was God. If *he* stopped working, they reasoned, the universe would spin out of control. Jesus justifies his actions by using the very argument they used to justify God's working on the Sabbath. He is saying, 'But you don't have a problem with God's working on the Sabbath, so why do you have a problem with my working on the Sabbath?'

The Jewish leaders see exactly what Jesus is driving at.

> For this reason the Jews tried all the harder to kill him; not only was he breaking the Sabbath, but he was even calling God his own Father, making himself equal with God. (5:18)

Jesus is saying and doing things that imply he is equal with God.

To a Jew, brought up on the fact that there is only one God, his claim is not only blasphemous, but baffling. What exactly does Jesus mean?

THE MIRACLE POINTS TO THE FACT THAT JESUS IS GOD'S SON CARRYING OUT HIS FATHER'S PLAN

The first point that Jesus wants them to understand is that he is not claiming to be a rival God come to work out an alternative plan of salvation for humankind. He is the Son who has come to implement his Father's plan.

> Jesus gave them this answer: 'I tell you the truth, the Son can do nothing by himself; he can do only what he sees his Father

doing, because whatever the Father does the Son also does. For the Father loves the Son and shows him all he does.' (5:19–20)

The Father and the Son are not operating independently of one another. The picture Jesus paints is of a family business. The father is, say, a potter, and because he loves his son, he delights to share with him all that he knows about making pots. He sits his son on his knee and shows him how to work the clay. And when the son grows up, he doesn't launch out on his own. He takes his place in the family pottery and makes the pots that his father tells him to make, in the way that he learned from his father.

When Jesus says that 'the Son can do nothing by himself', he means that he has not come to launch out on his own. What he has come to do all flows out of the fact that his Father loves him and has given him this work to do. And he, in turn, loves his Father, so he delights in pleasing him by doing the work that his Father has given him to do. He says that 'he can only do what he sees his Father doing'. In other words, whatever he does, he has learnt it from his Father. This means that, when we look at Jesus, we don't see a rival God. We see the Son, come to do the work of salvation that the Father has given him to do.

Hold on, you think. Doesn't that mean Jesus is in fact *inferior* to the Father? Doesn't that make him just another prophet, come to share his experience of God with us?

Look again at what Jesus said in verse 19: 'Whatever the Father does, the Son also does.' The authorities are thinking, 'But the Father has the power to make the stars.' And Jesus is saying, 'I can do whatever the Father can do. I can make stars.' The authorities are thinking, 'But the Father has power to forgive, and heal people and raise them from the dead and ...' And Jesus insists, '*Whatever* the Father does, I can do.' This miracle is another one of the signs that John records because it points to who Jesus is. The Sabbath was a day that was all about God reviving his people. John wants us to look at this miracle and ask, 'What sort of person gives new life to people on a Sabbath. Isn't that the sort of thing that only God can do?' And that is the point that Jesus is making. '*Whatever* God can do, I can do.'

If I had been Elvis' agent, I could have planned his schedule of concerts for him and negotiated contracts on his behalf, and in press conferences I could have even spoken for him. If anyone questioned what I was doing, I could have said something like, 'What I am telling you is straight from Elvis himself. I do nothing of my own accord. I do and say only what Elvis tells me to do and say.' But if I had stood up and said, 'In fact, whatever Elvis can do, I can do', everyone would have laughed. Did I mean that I could do the voice, the lips, the hips and everything Elvis did? Did I mean that if Elvis was ill I could stand in and nobody would notice? Nobody would want their money back?

But that is the kind of claim Jesus makes. He is not claiming to be just an agent, speaking on behalf of God. Rather, he is saying, 'Whatever God can do, I can do.'

In this chapter we are looking – through a different window – at the same view that John started his Gospel with. Jesus is not just another man sent by God. He is claiming a unique relationship with God. He is saying, 'The reason I say what I say, and do what I do, is because I am the

Son of God and I have come from my Father to carry out his plan to put this whole world back together again.'

What do you make of a claim like that?

WEIGHING UP THE CLAIM THAT JESUS MAKES

You may have come across the idea that passages such as the one we find in John 5 were invented much later by the church and have no basis in the life of the historical Jesus. The weakness of that theory is that there is no evidence for a primitive Christianity in which Jesus was just a good man who called for the religion of the day to be less formal and more heartfelt. The very first Christians were gripped by the conviction that, through Jesus, God was bringing his plan of salvation to its climax. From the very start, Jews who had been brought up to worship no one but the Lord their God saw that the only way to respond to Jesus was to worship him as God. But, you may ask, were those first Christians right to come to the conclusions they did about Jesus?

Let's look at three incidents that form part of Jesus' core ministry.

Overturning the tables in the temple

When Jesus storms into the temple courts and overturns the tables of those who were buying and selling (2:13–22), his action is often assumed to be part of his call for the religious establishment to stop trying to make money out of the poor. But he doesn't just call for the worship in the temple to be cleaned up. He pronounces God's judgment on the whole temple system. Not only that, but he claims that if people want to be restored to God, they should stop going to the temple and start coming to him. What sort of good man stands up and says that he has come to replace the system of worship that God had given his people? What sort of good man says, 'If you want to worship God, you need to check in with me first'?

Riding into Jerusalem on a donkey

You and I might not think that there was anything particularly controversial about the fact that Jesus rode into Jerusalem on a donkey (12:12–18). But the crowds recognized that Jesus was self-consciously fulfilling one of the ancient prophecies. They hailed him as the long-promised King, come to save God's people. This was not a fictitious incident that was pasted in later by the church. It was a public event that gave momentum to the historical reasons for the authorities seeing Jesus as a threat and wanting to kill him. If Jesus was just a good man launching a less hierarchical religious movement, it is hard to understand why he appointed himself King.

The Last Supper

The Passover was a Jewish festival that looked back at how, centuries earlier, God had saved his people from Egypt and looked forward to the day when God would come and set his people free again. At the last supper that Jesus shared with his disciples, he took some bread and wine and explained that the bread stood for his body and the wine for his blood. All that the Passover pointed to would be fulfilled by his body being broken and his blood shed on a cross. To make sure his disciples did not miss the significance of this, he didn't just say it in words. He acted it out with symbols that they would never forget. What sort of good man looks you in the eye and claims that all the hopes of God's people are going to reach their climax in his death?

JESUS CAME TO DO WHAT ONLY GOD COULD DO

The first Christians claimed that Jesus had come to bring God's plans for this world to their climax. That claim does not hinge on one or two quotations from Jesus that they might have misunderstood. It is the conclusion that the whole shape of his ministry points to. By his words and his deeds Jesus was making it clear that he was the one everyone had been waiting for. He had come to bring God's promises in the Old Testament to their climax.

If you fillet this claim out of the Gospels (by saying that it too was just the invention of the early Christians), then it is hard to make any historical sense of why Jesus was killed by the authorities. The sort of 'good man' that most people nowadays think Jesus was might have slightly irritated the religious authorities, but wouldn't have threatened them. The authorities saw the direction that the signs were pointing only too clearly. By what he said and did, Jesus was claiming that they were no longer at the centre of God's purposes, but that he was. It was a direct threat to their role and so to their very existence.

JESUS IS THE SON OF GOD

The question for us is this: what sort of man goes round putting himself at the centre of God's purposes for the whole world? If I stood up and said that in my life I was bringing God's plan of salvation for this world to its climax, what would you think of me? You might think I was evil. You might think I was ill. But you would not think that I was good.

Here is the puzzle that we have to get our heads around if we are to get to grips with Jesus. Everything we know about him points to his being good, and yet everything we know about him points to the fact that he was making a claim that no good man would ever make.

The reason why the first Christians never preached that 'Jesus was a good man whose example you should follow' was because that was the one conclusion you could not draw from his ministry. The whole shape of his ministry pointed to the fact that he had come to bring salvation to the whole world. In other words, he had come to do what the Old Testament said only God could do. If you are talking about someone who is doing what only God can do, what sort of language do you have to use about that person? It is no surprise that the first Christians used the sort of language that people normally used of God. It is no surprise that they realized that the only way to respond to Jesus was not merely to respect, but to worship him.

Let's go back to John 5. Our question was, 'What gives Jesus the authority to say that he alone can give us the life with God that we need?' Jesus' answer in John 5 is that he has God's authority, because he is God's Son come to carry out God's plan for this world.

This breathtaking claim cannot be dismissed as an isolated soundbite. When we look at the whole shape of

Jesus' ministry, what we see is that it all points to the same conclusion. This healing is just one of the many signs that point to who Jesus is. And what Jesus goes on to say is that this miracle sheds particular light on what it will mean for him to carry out God's plan for the world. The fact that he raises the paralysed man and warns him about judgment points to two things: to the fact that Jesus will raise the dead and the fact that Jesus will judge the world.

JESUS WILL RAISE THE DEAD

> For just as the Father raises the dead and gives them life, even so the Son gives life to whom he is pleased to give it. (5:21)

The man lying by the pool is a picture of each one of us. Because of his sin, he has no hope of life. He exists. But it is not the life that he was created for. This man's paralysis is a poignant reminder that he has walked out on God. And when we walk out on the God of life, our days are shot through with death. We are like cut flowers, beautiful for a time, but every petal that withers and falls to the floor is a reminder that the flowers have been cut off from their life-source. Like the petals on the floor, the sickness and suffering in our lives remind us that we have been cut off from our life-source. Death is not something that will happen to us one day in the future. It is something that is already happening to us. And, as with cut flowers, it is just a matter of time until we are removed from the vase altogether. In the meantime we can try anything we like: lose weight, eat more spinach, have our teeth whitened, dye our hair and swim three times a week, but none of it amounts to more than sticking the fallen petals back on the flowers. We try to wriggle out of the grip that death has on us, but our only hope is to be reconnected to the God who is the source of our life. Watering the whale eases its pain, but its only hope of life is to be restored to the ocean.

The Jews knew this, and that is why they looked forward to the day when God would come and fulfil his promises. In his love, God promised that he would not leave his people to the consequences of their sin. Just as Jesus didn't leave this man by the pool, God will not abandon his people to the grave. When he comes to put this whole world right, he will raise the dead and restore his people to the life they were created for.

If you have had to watch someone whom you love die, you will know how utterly helpless you feel. You would do anything to be able to turn back death's relentless march. But there is nothing you can do. Life is not ours to give. But Jesus says these remarkable words:

> For as the Father has life in himself, so he has granted the Son to have life in himself. (5:26)

By saying that he has 'life in himself', Jesus is claiming that he is not merely borrowing life for a time – as we are. He is the *source* of life. And as the one who is the source of life, he is the one who is able to give us the life that we need. Raising this paralysed man points to what Jesus will one day do. A few chapters on, those claims are given further substance when he raises a man called Lazarus from the dead.

Why should this man take Jesus seriously? Why should we? Because he is claiming to speak with authority on a subject on which you and I have no answers. He is claiming to be the source of the life that cut flowers like us desperately need to be restored to. On the day that God makes this whole world new and the dead are raised to life with God for ever, Jesus claims that he will be the one raising the dead and giving them life.

On the lips of anyone else it would be laughable. But Jesus is the Son of God, who has come from his Father to carry out God's plan of salvation. On *his* lips it is music to our ears. Death leaves so much unfulfilled and unfinished. It leaves things unsaid and unresolved. It separates us from all the people we love. But in the story of our lives, death is not the final word. Jesus is.

> *But in the story of our lives, death is not the final word. Jesus is.*

And he promises to take all that is broken and put it back together again.

And it's not just that Jesus is claiming to be the one who will raise the dead on the future day when God makes this whole world new.

I tell you the truth, whoever hears my word and believes him who sent me has eternal life and will not be condemned; he has crossed over from death to life. (5:24)

Jesus says that whoever responds to him '*has* eternal life' and '*has* crossed over from death to life'. Eternal life starts today. Jesus can give us this life that starts today and lasts for ever because he can give us a relationship with God that starts today and lasts for ever. If we turn to Jesus today, our bodies will, of course, still wither and die and will need to be raised up when God makes all things new. But on the day that we all stand before God, those who have responded to Jesus today will 'not be condemned'. They will not stand before God as his enemies, who cannot come in, but as old friends whom God will welcome home. So, when we walk into the world made new, it won't be the *beginning* of eternal life. It will be like getting married. It will be the consummation of a relationship that has already started.

JESUS WILL JUDGE THE WORLD

The Jews looked forward to a day when God would come to judge the world. We flinch at the idea of a God who judges. And yet, curiously, we all long for justice. Whether it is a story of political oppression or of a young man murdered for his mobile phone, when we watch the news on the TV something in us longs for justice to be done. We long for a world where everything is put right. But putting things right means dealing with all that is wrong. It means judgment. Jesus says to us, 'Good news: just as death will not have the last word, evil will not triumph.' Justice will be done because there is a judge in heaven. The shock in these verses is not that Jesus is talking about a day of judgment, but that he is saying that *he is the judge*.

Moreover, the Father judges no-one, but has entrusted all judgment to the Son. (5:22)

The Old Testament had pointed to the fact that at the centre of God's final judgment there would be a figure called 'the Son of Man'. He was a human figure who was to be given God's authority to judge the world. And Jesus claims to be that 'Son of Man':

For as the Father has life in himself, so he has granted the Son to have life in himself. And he has given him authority to judge because he is the Son of Man. (5:26–27)

When my wife put me in charge of tidying our garden shed, it meant fixing up some shelves, banging in nails from which to hang trowels and spanners, sorting screws into jamjars and cleaning the barbecue. But it also meant throwing things away. I got rid of a pile of broken flowerpots and half-used paint tins and a roll of rusty wire netting.

God has put Jesus in charge of making the whole world new. It will mean fixing things that are broken, straightening things out and tidying up the mess. But there will also be things that he will have to get rid of. The sort of things that we see on the news and that break our hearts will have no place in the new world. Which means there are people who will have no place in the new world.

Giving life and giving judgment are two sides of the same coin. Putting all things right will mean dealing with all that is wrong. This is good news for our world, but it is also very sobering news. If Jesus is going to deal with all that is wrong, how will he deal with me?

We saw back in chapter 4 that being right in God's eyes is not about being better than other people. It is about treating God as God. Listen to what Jesus says about what it means to treat God as God.

> Moreover, the Father judges no-one, but has entrusted all judgment to the Son, that all may honour the Son just as they honour the Father. He who does not honour the Son does not honour the Father, who sent him. (5:22–23)

If I am to honour God as God, that will mean honouring his Son. I cannot say that I am right with God if I am not honouring the Son, whom he sent in order to put me into a right relationship with him. Jesus is saying that our eternal destiny all hinges on how we treat him.

If we have assumed that he was just a good teacher from two thousand years ago, then it is very easy to ignore him. But if he is God's appointed judge – if my eternal destiny hangs on his verdict on my life – then I cannot afford to ignore him.

✢ ✢ ✢

Perhaps you can see that the stakes are high. Perhaps you are beginning to think that this is something you want to look into further. But your days are just packed. In the light of your 'to do' list, it is hard to see when you are going to get round to it, because although, in theory, the whole question of who Jesus is sounds important, in practice it just doesn't feel all that relevant.

Chapter 8

BREAD FOR THE JOURNEY
John 6:1–59

Some time after this, Jesus crossed to the far shore of the Sea of Galilee (that is, the Sea of Tiberias), and a great crowd of people followed him because they saw the miraculous signs he had performed on the sick. Then Jesus went up on a mountainside and sat down with his disciples. The Jewish Passover Feast was near.

When Jesus looked up and saw a great crowd coming towards him, he said to Philip, 'Where shall we buy bread for these people to eat?' He asked this only to test him, for he already had in mind what he was going to do.

Philip answered him, 'Eight months' wages would not buy enough bread for each one to have a bite!'

Another of his disciples, Andrew, Simon Peter's brother, spoke up, 'Here is a boy with five small barley loaves and two small fish, but how far will they go among so many?' (6:9).

The crowd have followed Jesus up into the hills and, as the day wears on, they grow hungry. So Jesus, ever alive to people's needs, tells his disciples to go and buy some food for them. All five thousand of them.

'You've got to be kidding!' says Philip. 'It would take a small fortune to feed this lot.'

Andrew, clutching at straws, volunteers a small boy's packed lunch.

But Jesus says, 'Great. Get everyone sitting down. Let's eat.'

You can imagine how foolish the disciples feel. There are five thousand people and between them they have five loaves and two small fish, and Jesus asks his disciples to share these round. But somehow the loaves and fish never run out. The people eat their fill and there are twelve full baskets left over:

> When they had all had enough to eat, he said to his disciples, 'Gather the pieces that are left over. Let nothing be wasted.' So they gathered them and filled twelve baskets with the pieces of the five barley loaves left over by those who had eaten. (6:12–13)

This is big. In a country in which people spend their days working the land just to get enough food to survive, someone who can feed five thousand people with five loaves and two small fish has a lot of power. A whisper goes round the crowd.

> After the people saw the miraculous sign that Jesus did, they began to say, 'Surely this is the Prophet who is to come into the world.' (6:14)

They wonder if Jesus could be the one they have been waiting for to lead them in a revolution against the Romans. John says that Jesus, 'knowing that they intended to come and make him king by force, withdrew again to a mountain by himself' (6:15).

The next day, some of the crowd catch up with Jesus and plead with him. 'Jesus, what are you doing over here? You should be back there, with the people. They want you to lead them.' And you'd think Jesus would be pleased. After his run-in with the authorities, here at last are people who believe in him.

But it turns out that they don't believe in Jesus at all. Jesus answers, 'I tell you the truth, you are looking for me, not because you saw miraculous signs but because you ate the loaves and had your fill' (6:26).

The feeding of the five thousand was another sign. But the crowd didn't see what it pointed to. All they saw was a man who could feed an army. So Jesus says to them:

> Do not work for food that spoils, but for food that endures to eternal life, which the Son of Man will give you. On him God the Father has placed his seal of approval. (6:27)

Just as Jesus spoke about physical water and spiritual water, he now says that there are two types of food. There is 'food that spoils' and 'food that endures to eternal life'. 'Food that spoils' nourishes our physical needs. It keeps us going from day to day, but it cannot give us spiritual life. 'Food that endures to eternal life' is food that nourishes us spiritually.

It gives us the life that Jesus has been talking about, that starts now and lasts for ever.

If you asked a member of the crowd to articulate their greatest need in life, they would say food for the table. So, for as long as they think Jesus has come to throw off the yoke of Roman oppression and lead them out of poverty into a more comfortable life, they are all ears. But when he tells them that he has come to bring food for eternity rather than food for the table, they lose interest. John records that 'from this time many of his disciples turned back and no longer followed him' (6:66).

WHAT IS OUR GREATEST NEED?

It may be that you can relate to the crowd. Eternal life sounds like pie in the sky in the face of the very real needs that press down on you here and now. If you are weighed down by debt, the chances are that it doesn't feel like you need Jesus, it feels like you need a job. If you are exhausted, it is not Jesus you are longing for, but a holiday. If work is overwhelming you, unless Jesus can get you an extension to your essay deadline, he doesn't look as though he is in any position to help you. We tell ourselves that once everything else has settled down we will make time to look into the whole question of eternal life, but right now our hands are full with the challenge thrown up by today. But this is the thing: if we weigh up our needs purely in the light of here and now, it is very hard to identify what our needs really are.

It is like packing for a holiday. If I were to tell you that tomorrow I was taking you on an all-expenses-paid holiday of a lifetime, in order to pack for it you would need to know where we were going. What you would pack for the mountains would be very different from what you would pack for the beach. So if I don't tell you the destination, you won't know whether to pack flipflops or skis. You won't know whether you need a sleeping bag or a mosquito net.

If we don't know where we are heading to in eternity, it is very hard to know what to fill our days with, because we can't see what we really need. So we end up packing flipflops *and* snow boots. We cram our days with everything we can lay our hands on. We put in long days at work, mornings in the gym and nights on the town. For our holidays we are going scuba diving and in between everything else we play in a band and we are learning to speak Spanish and we're hoping to shoot a movie and put down decking in the garden. And, from a distance, it looks like a whole load of fun. But inside we know that the fun is wearing a bit thin, because we're not sure what we are packing for. So we keep cramming in more and we swing from high days, when we feel we have everything, to low days, when all that we have doesn't seem to add up to anything.

Jesus says that, in the light of eternity, more than anything else in our lives we need him.

We saw in the last chapter that history is heading to a day when each one of us will stand before the Judge and give an account of our lives. Those who have honoured Jesus will be invited into the new creation. Those who did not will be shut out.

If I said that the holiday I was taking you on was a skiing holiday, you wouldn't spend tomorrow frantically searching for your swimming trunks. You would know that we were not going to need them. In the light of the destination you would know to fill your bag with woolly hats and thermal vests. Jesus says that, in the light of eternity, more than anything else in our lives we need him.

JESUS IS OUR GREATEST NEED

'I am the bread of life', he says (6:35). The trouble is that, as an image, 'bread' doesn't do it for us.

I love bread. But if you asked me to draw up a list of my greatest needs, it would never cross my mind to put down 'bread'. I have never woken up worrying that I might not get the bread I need to survive the day. Within a ten-minute walk of my front door there are three bakeries. At the drop of a hat I could get my hands on a granary roll, a bagel, a baguette, a ciabatta or even a walnut loaf. In the Western world we don't think of bread as something we *need*. It is something we just have. In abundance. Ask us why we go to work, and it never occurs to us to say, 'So that we can buy bread.' We talk about being 'breadwinners', but what motivates us at work is the prospect of promotion and a higher salary, so that we can buy a new kitchen and go on more foreign holidays – not the prospect of *bread*. Bread is not the reason we get out of bed in the morning. Bread is just what we put in the toaster before we head out to work. In our lives, bread is just assumed.

But in much of the world the reason for going to work is simple. You work because you need bread. In some cultures, the equivalent might be rice or yams. But the need for bread looms large over every day, because without it you will die. Jesus is talking to people who know what it means to need bread. And he says, '*I* am the bread that you need. Without me, you will die.'

In order to hear the full force of Jesus' claim to be the bread of life, we need to tune in to the Old Testament background to what Jesus is saying. Back in the Old Testament, God rescued his people from slavery in Egypt in order to lead them to a land in which they would be free to worship him and enjoy the riches of life with him as their God. It was a mouth-watering prospect. But not long into their journey through the desert, it looked as though God's promise was going to come to nothing. Their provisions ran out, and the people turned on Moses, who was leading them. 'Whose stupid idea was this, then, to lead us out into the desert? There is no way we will make it to this Promised Land. We were better off back in Egypt. At least we had food in Egypt!' But God assures his people that he will not let them die. He will get them to the Promised Land. They won't starve, because he himself will provide for them. So every day, as they travelled through the desert, the Lord provided them with bread that they called 'manna'.

And now the crowd have caught up with Jesus and want him to do another miracle, like the one their forefathers witnessed in the desert. They want Jesus to produce some more manna. But Jesus explains that he has not come just to repeat the miracle, he has come to fulfil all that the miracle pointed to. God is now giving the 'true bread ... [that] gives life to the world' (6:32–33). The bread in the desert gave life to Israel, but it pointed to the fact that one day God would give the 'true bread' that would give life to the whole world.

The people listening are keen to have some of it, so they ask Jesus, 'Give us this true bread.' And that is when Jesus says, 'I am the bread of life' (6:34–35).

God gave bread from heaven to get Israel to the Promised Land. Without it they would never have got there. But the bread gave them life. Jesus is claiming to be the 'true bread'. God has given Jesus from heaven not just to get Israel to the Promised Land, but to get the whole world into God's promised new creation. Without him we will never get there. He is our only hope of life.

IF WE DON'T HAVE JESUS WE DON'T HAVE LIFE

Several years ago, my mother organized a family reunion in Germany to celebrate my grandmother's eightieth birthday. The boat had been pushed out a very long way, and my mother – who doesn't do things by halves – hired a people carrier, so that we could travel to Germany in air-conditioned comfort. She had made enough food to ensure that in the event of world war we could just park the people carrier and see it through on a diet of bacon-and-egg rolls, chicken wings, pasta salads, potato salad, fizzy drinks and yoghurts. Each of us had our own personal bag for rubbish and a little packet of handy travel wipes for sticky fingers. She had also brought along two portable CD players, so that we could listen to the music of our choice.

In the queue at Dover, there was a bloke behind us leaning up against his car. I am not good at cars, but I think it was blue and slightly rusty. He was dunking a Mars bar into a plastic cup of coffee he had bought at the café.

Of the two vehicles, which do you think had what it needed for the journey?

Then it came to finding the passports. Mum started pulling things out of her bag, rooting around in the glove compartment, shaking all the coats and even unpacking the rolls. She couldn't find the passports. *Now* which of the two vehicles do you think had what it needed for the journey? We couldn't pay off passport control with a pork pie.

After hot tears and twenty minutes unpacking the entire people carrier, the passports were eventually found in a side pocket. But it was a sharp reminder of what you really need when you are going on a journey. In the light of passport control, all the potato salad in the world is irrelevant. What you really need is your passport.

In the light of the fact that one day we are going to stand before our Judge, all the Italian shoes in the world are irrelevant. What you really need is bread to give you life with God.

What is it that you feel that you most need right now? Before you pack it into your suitcase, it is worth asking if it really is what you most need for the journey. The question is not just 'Will it get you through life?' but 'Will it get you through death?' Jesus is not for one moment saying that a job or a holiday or a roof over your head or a square meal aren't important human needs. He made sure that the five thousand who were hungry had more than enough to eat.

But the danger is that we think that these things are the sum of our needs, and so we cram our suitcase so full with 'bread that spoils' that there isn't room for the 'true bread'.

Until we have faced up to death we will never face up to what we really need in life. But when small children ask us about death we don't know what to say, because we don't much like to think about it. Which means that when we crash into death it is like running into a glass wall. We don't see it coming and so we are not ready for it.

Today we may feel that Jesus is just a comfort blanket for the sort of people who don't have much else in their suitcase to console them. We don't like to think of ourselves as the sort of people who need him, because we like to think that our lives are brimming over, our bags packed full with family and friends and a whole load of fun. But on the day we go crashing into the glass wall, the bags we have packed for eternity will feel horribly empty. We may well have lived a little. But we never had life.

JESUS IS THE BREAD THAT WILL GET US TO THE PROMISED LAND

> I am the bread of life. He who comes to me will never go hungry, and he who believes in me will never be thirsty. (6:35)

Without Jesus, we will die. With him, we will never go hungry.

When he says that we will 'never go hungry', he is not promising that we will pass all our exams, have a beautiful family, get to the top of the ladder and never fall ill. For the people of Israel, it would have been easier in some ways to have stayed in Egypt. In Egypt they had food and shelter. Jesus says that following him is not the safe and comfortable option. He goes on to warn his disciples that 'if they persecuted me, they will persecute you also' (15:20). When Jesus calls us, he calls us to follow him on an adventure that could take us across some rocky terrain. Depending on where in the world you live, following Jesus could mean that you are laughed at, disowned by your family, marked down in your essays, sacked from your job, thrown into prison or killed. Like the Israelites, we will be tempted to look back at those who, as it were, stayed in Egypt and envy them their comfort.

For the people of Israel as they travelled across the desert, there were happy days and dark days: days when they celebrated, days when they had to bury their dead, days when they made good progress and days when they thought they would never get there. But there was never a day on which they went hungry. Every day there was bread from heaven. Every day God was with them, sustaining them on their journey. And he did not let them go. He got them to the Promised Land. And that is the promise that Jesus makes to us.

> All that the Father gives me will come to me, and whoever comes to me I will never drive away. For I have come down from heaven not to do my will but to do the will of him who sent me. And this is the will of him who sent me, that I shall lose none of all that he has given me, but raise them up at the last day. (6:37–39)

Jesus promises us that if we turn to him he will never let go of us. He has come do his Father's will. And his Father's will is that Jesus should be the bread for us, every day, giving us the life we need to get us safely in to the promised land of the world made new.

Since becoming a Christian I have known many sunny days. But I have also known dark days, when I have messed up, or people have hurt me, or plans have fallen through. But although I have known what it is to be bitterly disappointed, I have never been disappointed by Jesus.

In 1824 Adonirum Judson was thrown into a Burmese prison and tortured. He was cut off from his family, his home, his work and every comfort. All the things that we think of as giving us life were ripped out of his hands. And yet he was able to testify that even in prison, with iron fetters around his ankles, he still had life, because he still had Jesus. He wrote:

> It is all one whether [a Christian] is in the city or a desert, among relations or among savage foes, in the heat of the Indies or in the ice of Greenland; his infinite Friend is always at hand. He need not fear want or sickness or pain, for his best Friend does all things well. He need not fear death, though it come in the most shocking form, for death is only the withdrawing of the veil which conceals his dearest Friend.

Jesus is the true bread. If we turn to him, he will give us the life that we need. All other bread spoils. It keeps us going for a leg or two of the journey, but it doesn't last. But Jesus will nourish us for all eternity. He is bread that will never spoil, or fade, or rust. He won't get stolen, or end in divorce. We can't get fired from him, illness won't ruin him and even death can't snatch him away. Every day he will be there for us: our food for the journey and our strength to go on. And he will not lose us. He will lead us through this world and then raise us up into a world made new.

That is why he assures us that 'he who believes has everlasting life' (6:47). If we believe in him, we have the life that we need. But what does it mean to believe in Jesus?

BELIEVING IN JESUS MEANS FEEDING ON JESUS

If I come back from the shops with a freshly baked white crusty loaf under my arm, I can have it in the house and store it in the bread bin for as long as I like, but it won't do me any good until I eat it. To believe in Jesus means to feed on him.

> I am the living bread that came down from heaven. If anyone eats of this bread, he will live for ever. This bread is my flesh, which I will give for the life of the world. (6:51)

The crowd are as puzzled as we are. 'How can this man give us his flesh to eat?' they ask (6:52).

Jesus is not calling them to cannibalism. What he is saying is that the way he gives us life is not by being a good teacher, or a miracle worker, or by being a wonderful role model for us all. The way he gives us life is by dying. On the cross he will give his flesh 'for the life of the world'.

For us to live, other things have to die. If we are going to eat sausages and chips, then pigs and potatoes have to die. It is the same with bread. If there is going to be bread, then wheat has to die. You could say that the wheat dies in order to bring life to the people who eat the bread. And that is the picture that Jesus is drawing. He is saying that his death will bring us life. He will go on to explain more of *how* his death brings life to the world, and we will reflect on what he says in a later chapter. But for now, he is telling us how to approach his death. He is telling us to approach it like a starving man would approach a loaf of bread in the desert. To a starving man, a loaf of bread is not an irrelevance. It is not just an interesting idea that he will bear in mind and get round to looking into some day. He wouldn't just tear a bit off and put it in his pocket for good luck, nor would he just be inspired or moved by it. He would bite into it as one whose life depended on it.

There are plenty of people who have read books on Jesus, or who enjoy singing hymns about Jesus, or listening to sermons about Jesus, but who are still hungry. That is because they have put the bread of life in the bread bin and left him there. Bread won't do you any good unless you eat it. Jesus says we are to feed on him as people whose lives depend on him.

This is what it means to believe in Jesus. It means to turn to him as a starving man turns to a loaf of bread and say, 'You are my only hope of life. Without you I will die.'

And if you turn to him, he promises that he will never drive you away or let you go. You will be able to say, 'I was starving to death, but now I never go hungry. I knew nothing of God in my life, now he is always with me, day by day. And whatever happens, I have a future to look forward to, a future with him in a world made new.'

✢   ✢   ✢

We need Jesus more than anything else, because he is the bread that will get us to our journey's end. But what is it like to put ourselves in his hands?

Chapter 9

LIFE TO THE FULL
John 10:1–21

Jesus says, 'I am the good shepherd' (10:11).

And we tune right out. You see, we don't need a shepherd, because we are not sheep.

I mean, if you were to think of yourself as an animal, what animal would you be? A lion? An eagle? An owl? I've never heard anyone say, 'Actually, I like to think of myself as a sheep.'

No, we like to think of ourselves as strong and free and wise: masters of our own destiny, captains of our soul, boldly beating down our own path through this world. In our minds we are so in the driving seat. In reality, we are so driven.

The ancient Greeks knew this. They saw that nearly everything that is most important in our lives is something that happens to us, rather than something that we make happen: the country we are born in, the family situation we are born into, the culture we are steeped in, the people who influence us. The fact is that we are all followers, swept along by a flow of circumstances and experiences and ideas and people. Even our best attempts to swim against the tide are strangely conformist.

I was a teenager in the mid-1980s. At our school your hair at the back wasn't allowed to touch your collar. So we grew our fringes right down to our chins. It meant you had to tilt your head and look at the teachers sideways – which somehow felt defiant. We wore baggy trousers with pleated fronts and had them taken in at the ankles so tightly you had to get up early to give yourself time to pull them on in the mornings. And what we thought we were doing was rebelling against school uniform. In reality, all we were doing was dressing up in another uniform, one that we'd all picked up from a band called The Smiths.

God says that the animal that best expresses our experience of being human is a sheep. We are all sheep. And we all have shepherds. We all have people who tell us what is cool and what is uncool, what is right and what is wrong, people who teach us how to think, how to feel and what to live for. If we have answers, none of us has thought them up by ourselves. We learned them from the people who have shaped us. Shepherded us, in fact. People who were themselves shepherded by others.

The question we need to ask is, 'Are these shepherds who shape our lives any good?' You see, it matters.

As far as I can tell, if you and I were real sheep and we lived in a country like England, it wouldn't matter a whole lot how good our shepherd was. In most parts of England there is plenty of rain, which means there is plenty of grass, and there are no wolves. And so, on the whole, a shepherd could just stick us in a field and leave us to it.

But in the Middle East, if you were a sheep your whole life depended on your shepherd being a *good* shepherd. The owner of a flock of sheep would hire a shepherd to look after his sheep. The shepherd's job was to lead the sheep to water and pasture – which, in the long, hot summers, were hard to find. Would your shepherd know where to lead you for nourishment? Along the way you would travel across rocky terrain. If you fell behind, or slipped, or got caught in a thicket, would he be the sort of shepherd who'd come after you? If wolves attacked you, would he just run away, or would he stay and fight? If you were a sheep, your life depended on your shepherd.

Now, come back to what Jesus is saying about himself in John 10:11: 'I am the good shepherd.' In verse 16 he adds, 'I have other sheep that are not of this sheep pen. I must bring them also.' Jesus is saying that he is not just the shepherd of the Jewish people. He is saying that people of all nations are his sheep. He is saying, 'Whoever you are, wherever you are from, your life depends on me. I am the shepherd you need.'

It is a crazy claim. You and I have our work cut out caring for our family and perhaps a close circle of friends. But, calm as you like, Jesus says he is the shepherd of all the sheep in all the world. If you were listening to Jesus with Jewish ears, his words would have rung all kinds of bells.

In the Old Testament God spoke of his people Israel as his sheep. He had, as it were, hired the leaders of Israel to shepherd his sheep for him. But again and again they had neglected his sheep, and the upshot was that Jerusalem was attacked and God's people were carted off into exile in Babylon. The flock was scattered.

The Bible claims that the history of Israel holds a mirror up to the whole of humanity. We are all sheep, we have all been scattered. We all, like sheep, have turned away from God and wandered off down paths that have left us lost and a long way from home. What we need is a good shepherd to come and find us and lead us back to the safety of God's care.

Back in the Old Testament, this is what the Lord says to his scattered people:

> For this is what the Sovereign LORD says: I myself will search for my sheep and look after them. As a shepherd looks after his scattered flock when he is with them, so will I look after my sheep. I will rescue them from all the places where they were scattered on a day of clouds and darkness. I will bring them out from the nations and gather them from the countries, and I will bring them into their own land. I will pasture them on the mountains of Israel, in the ravines and in all the settlements in the land. I will tend them in a good pasture, and the mountain heights of Israel will be their grazing land. There they will lie down in good grazing land, and there they will feed in a rich pasture on the mountains of Israel. I myself will tend my sheep and have them lie down, declares the Sovereign LORD. I will search for the lost and bring back the strays. I will bind up the injured and strengthen the weak, but the sleek and the strong I will destroy. I will shepherd the flock with justice. (Ezekiel 34:11–16)

The hired shepherds have neglected the sheep. So, in his love, God promises that he will himself come and be the Good Shepherd his people so desperately need. He will come and 'search for the lost' and 'bind up the injured and strengthen the weak'. It was a day that his people longed for.

And Jesus stands up and says, 'I am *that* shepherd. I am God come to seek out my lost sheep scattered across the face of the whole world.' In chapter 8 we saw that to believe in Jesus means to feed on him as a starving man would feed on a loaf of bread. When Jesus says that he is the 'good shepherd', he is making a similar point. He is calling us to depend on him for our lives.

It is a call we instinctively turn our noses up at because it smells of weakness. In the event of being caught in the thicket of a personal crisis, it is good to know that this shepherd is there, on standby. But generally we like to pick our own way through the mountains. Living in a culture that has made a hero of the rugged individualist has left us a little ashamed of that fact that, secretly, we long for someone we could depend on. But at the dawn of creation, before things were spoilt, the first human beings depended on the Lord as their shepherd. That was not because they were weak, but because – as the whale was created for the sea – human beings were created to depend on God. We were not created for rugged individualism. We were created for relationship with God and relationship with one another. So Jesus is not a crutch for the weak. When he calls us to lean on him, he is calling us all to learn to be human again.

It might be that you are weighing up Jesus' call to lean on him, and you want to know what difference he will make to your life. As Jesus unfolds the image of the good shepherd, we get a picture of what it is like to be one of his sheep.

THE GOOD SHEPHERD KNOWS HIS SHEEP
Listen to what Jesus says.

> I tell you the truth, the man who does not enter the sheep pen by the gate, but climbs in by some other way, is a thief and a robber. The man who enters by the gate is the shepherd of his sheep. The watchman opens the gate for him, and the sheep listen to his voice. He calls his own sheep by name and leads them out. When he has brought out all his own, he goes on ahead of them, and his sheep follow him because they know his voice. (10:1–4)

In a village there would have been one large pen into which all the farmers would have put their sheep. All their flocks would be mixed in together. The farmers would then hire a watchman to look after all the sheep in the pen and to guard the gate against sheep rustlers. When the shepherd of one of the flocks came along, the watchman would open the gate for him. The shepherd would then give a distinctive kind of whistle, and his flock would recognize his call. They would all troop out, and he would then lead them off into the hills for pasture. The shepherd didn't show up and call out to the sheep in general, hoping that perhaps one or two might take an interest in him. He knew exactly which sheep were his and he came to call them out.

Jesus is saying that he has come for his sheep. And when he comes he doesn't just issue a general invitation, a sort of

'Sorry to interrupt, but I wonder if I can interest anyone in following me?' He knows his sheep by name. He says, 'Ruth, I'm here, I have come for you. John, I have come for you. Ravi, Tom, Chloe, I have come for you.' He 'calls his own sheep by name'. And a name is not just a label. When he says he knows our names, he means he knows who we are.

This is not merely omniscience. It's not that because he's God he knows all about us, as if he had a file on us. This is love. He is God, so to each one of his sheep he says, 'I know you. When you were being formed in your mother's womb, I knew you. When you took your first steps, my eyes were on you. I remember your first day at school. When your parents split up, I was there. When your father died, I was there with you. In your teen-age years, when nobody else understood what you were going through, I know just *Here is someone who knows who we really are.* how much it hurt. I know your sorrows and I know your joys. I know how much you love to climb mountains and surf. I know how much music means to you. And I know how they treat you at work – I have heard what they say. I know your hopes and dreams. I know who you really are.' Here is someone who knows who we really are.

We have friends who know us from college, but who know nothing about what we were like at school, or people with whom we go to the pub who would hardly recognize us at work. Our family have put us in a box, and every time they announce that 'She's always been rather serious' it hurts so much, because we know our friends love the way we make them laugh.

It makes your head spin. Sometimes you hardly know who you are yourself. You feel as if you are so many different people and you want to know which one is the real you. You long for someone who can pick up all the different fragments of your life and piece together your whole story – someone who knows everything about you because they have seen all that has happened to you and they understand how it has affected you. Someone, in other words, who can tell you who you really are.

And here he is. Jesus is not another stranger come barging into your life. He is the Shepherd God, and he says to you, 'I am the one you have been longing for. I know your whole story, I know who you are, and I have come to take care of you. Will you follow me?'

It is quite something to look up into the night sky and be able to say, 'I know the God who made the stars.' But to my mind, more amazing than the fact that we know him is that he knows us. Have you ever had that feeling at work that nobody really notices what you do? Rejoice in the fact that the God of the universe notices. Have you ever felt invisible at a party? Rejoice in the fact that God of the universe sees you. The world may barely know your name, but the God of the universe knows who you are. You are not just another obscure nobody. His eyes are on you, and he calls you 'mine'.

Politicians don't know our names. The bands we idolize have never heard of us. The footballers don't know us from

Adam. The columnists in the weekend papers have never met us. Our boss doesn't really know what makes us tick. And every Friday night, we would do anything to look good in the eyes of our friends, but all they do is put us under pressure to be someone we are not, because they don't know who we really are. Jesus says that sheep 'will never follow a stranger; in fact, they will run away from him because they do not recognise a stranger's voice' (10:5).

He is saying, 'Don't follow all these strangers. Don't let *strangers* tell you how to live. Don't march to the beat of their drum. Let me shepherd you.' Maybe you don't feel like listening to Jesus, because what does he know? He knows. He knows you better than you know yourself. Listen to him.

THE GOOD SHEPHERD GIVES LIFE TO HIS SHEEP

The people don't quite understand what Jesus is on about. So he explains: 'I tell you the truth, I am the gate for the sheep' (10:7). Which doesn't exactly clear things up. Jesus is a *gate*?

He is still using picture language from the world of sheep. Only now he is using it in a slightly different way. There is no grass in the pen, so, in order to live, the sheep need to be led from the pen and out to pasture. The only person who is entitled to open the gate and lead the sheep out to pasture is the shepherd.

But Jesus is saying, 'I am the one shepherd worth following, because I am the only one who can open the gate and lead you out into lush pasture.' But typically he says it is not just that he can open the gate, but that he *is* the gate.

If I were a sheep, I would spend my time in the pen gazing longingly at that gate, thinking, 'That gate is my way out to rich pasture.' That is how Jesus wants us to look at him. He wants us to see that he is our way out to life. His point is that he is the only shepherd who has a legitimate claim on us, and so the only shepherd who will lead us out to rich pasture. Anyone else is a thief who has climbed over the wall under the cover of darkness, and has come 'only to steal and kill and destroy' (10:10). Instead of taking the sheep out to pasture, the thief takes them straight to market.

Jesus is thinking of some of the nationalistic revolutionaries of his day, who promised to lead God's people into freedom. But the reality is that they 'steal and kill and destroy' the sheep. Like so many political leaders, they promised a new dawn, but all they could deliver was a sorry mess of bloodshed, tears and broken dreams. Jesus says, 'I have come that they may have life, and have it to the full' (10:10).

This is just about the opposite of what we think. Our working assumption is that just about everyone else offers life to the full. But not Jesus. We have marked Jesus down as the po-faced shepherd with sad eyes who will make our lives unbearably grey. Follow anyone, we think, but not Jesus, because following him will mean missing out on life.

It turns out we could not have got it more back to front. The very reason he came is to give us life in all its fullness. Like thirst needs water and hunger needs bread, sheep need grass and we need God.

If a sheep is going to enjoy life to the full, it needs a shepherd who will lead it to lush pasture. If we are going to enjoy life to the full, we need a shepherd who will lead us into a relationship with God. And that is exactly what Jesus came to do.

Notice that he doesn't just promise us 'life for ever' but 'life to the full'. That is to say, it is not merely a new quantity of life that Jesus promises us, but a new quality. 'Life to the full' within the world of sheep conjures up images of fat sheep feasting in contentment. This is not just more of the same old scrubland. This is rich and fertile pasture the like of which they have never experienced before.

As we have listened to Jesus in the pages of John's Gospel, he has made it very clear that the life that he brings is not just more of the same. Remember Nicodemus. The life that Jesus has come to bring is like being born again. Think of the radical difference between your experience of the world before you were born and after you were born. That is the kind of qualitative difference Jesus is talking about. And so that we don't miss the scale of the difference, remember the paralysed man by the pool. Jesus raised him up to show us that the difference he makes is the difference between being dead and being alive. The life that he brings is not a slightly more rounded version of the old life. It is a whole new life, because it is a whole new relationship with the God who made us. Once we were cut off from him. Now we have been restored to him. Once we were his enemies and now we are his friends.

Remember the woman at the well. Once we didn't know what it was to be loved, but now we know the love that quenches our deepest thirst. Once we lived for small gods who could not give us a big enough reason to be on this planet, but now we have found satisfaction in the God who is our reason for being on this planet. Once, we filled our lives with everything and anything, and it all felt so much like nothing, because we didn't know what it was all for. Now we know where we are going. And we have the bread that we need for the journey. And we know we will not get lost, because every day he is with us, sustaining us each step of the way. We have life because we have been restored to the God who is the source of our life.

As a boy, I inherited my great-grandfather's fishing tackle. There were about twenty different rods and a shed full of assorted gear, but I didn't really know what any of it was for, and there was no one around who could show me. That didn't dampen my enthusiasm. Just the smell of it all had me hooked. I persuaded my mother to take us all to a lake. One sunny afternoon we packed a picnic, and while the others climbed trees I went fly-fishing.

Now, you need to know that a fly-rod is light and whippy. With it you can cast a tiny fly out onto the water. A boat-rod is short and stiff. You use it to dangle heavy weights and big baits down into the depths of the ocean. On that sunny afternoon I went fly-fishing with a boat-rod. No matter how hard I tried, I couldn't get the fly more than about a yard out into the water. I spent most of my time untangling knots and yanking the hook out of weeds. But I enjoyed every minute of it. It was a happy afternoon. I decided that I just needed to practise my casting. Not long after that, a friend from school, whose father was a fisherman, told me what the different rods were for. It was then that I realized that all the practice in the world would have made no difference. I was using the wrong rod. In many ways it *was* a happy afternoon. But now I have tasted the real thing. I have cast a fly with a fly-rod and watched the line unfurl and the fly land softly on the water thirty yards upstream. Although I thought I was fly-fishing on that sunny afternoon, I now know that what I was doing didn't even come close to fly-fishing in all its fullness.

If we don't know the God who made us, we won't know what our lives are for. And, however hard we practise, we won't even come close to enjoying 'life to the full'. Living without God is like trying to cast a fly with a boat-rod. In many ways it can be a happy experience, but it is nothing compared with casting a fly with a fly-rod. Jesus restores us to the God who made us, and so sets us free to live the life that we were made for.

THE GOOD SHEPHERD LAYS DOWN HIS LIFE FOR THE SHEEP

> I am the good shepherd. The good shepherd lays down his life for the sheep. The hired hand is not the shepherd who owns the sheep. So when he sees the wolf coming, he abandons the sheep and runs away. Then the wolf attacks the flock and scatters it. (10:11–12)

At the first sign of a wolf, the hired hand legs it. He doesn't really care about the sheep, so he abandons them. Jesus, the true shepherd, sees the danger we are in and lays down his life to save us.

Throughout John's Gospel, Jesus has made it clear that when left to our own devices we don't have the sort of life with God that he has come to bring. We are sheep who have walked out on God. And the way we have treated him, his world and our fellow sheep means we are in danger. There is a danger of perishing. The wolf that we need protecting from is God's judgment.

That is why we need a need a good shepherd who won't abandon us in the face of that danger. And that is the sort of shepherd that the God of the Bible turns out to be. Jesus makes it clear that his death was neither an accident nor something that he was bullied into. He says, 'The reason my Father loves me is that I lay down my life – only to take it up again. No-one takes it from me, but I lay it down of my own accord' (10:17–18). In his love, the Father was willing to give up his dear Son to save us from the danger we were in. And in his love the Son came willingly.

I remember once reading about a soldier in the First World War. He had been wounded, and in hospital the doctor said to him, 'I am sorry you lost your arm.' To which the soldier replied, 'I didn't lose it. I gave it.' Jesus is saying that he is the Good Shepherd who chooses to *give* his life for his sheep.

And what makes the hairs on the back of my neck stand on end is that he says, 'I know my sheep ... and I lay down my life for the sheep' (10:14–15). It isn't that he just gave his life for sheep in general. He knew our names. He saw your face and my face and he saw the danger we were in, and because he loved not just people in general but you and me, he gave his life as a sacrifice for our sin to save us from the judgment that was coming our way.

That's how much we matter to him. That is how much he loves us.

It could be that, as you read this, you are quite close to getting up and following him, but there is something holding you back. You think of the people in your life who have let you down. And the experience has made you wary of depending on anyone. You tell yourself that you 'don't need God – or anyone else, for that matter'. But it's more that you don't want to get hurt again. And you wonder if Jesus is going to turn out to be no better than the rest of them. If that's you, look again at the sort of shepherd he is. He chose to lay down his life for you. That is how committed he is to your good. We won't always understand why this shepherd leads us along some of the paths that he does. But we can be sure that he is good, and that the journey he leads us on is always for our good. If we entrust ourselves to his care, he will not abuse that trust.

Perhaps you are hovering on the brink of committing yourself to him, but you've got half an eye on some of the other shepherds, who – quite frankly – look a better bet. Let me ask you: do you know any other shepherd who is prepared to lay down his life to save you? If you live for your career, would your boss die for you? If you live for what others think of you, would the friends whose opinion matters so much to you lay down their lives for you?

Jesus goes on to say that he lays down his life 'only to take it up again' (10:17). In other words, death could not hold him. This Good Shepherd is alive today, and he is calling people to follow him. How will you respond to his love for you? Will you come clean? Will you admit that you are not the lion, or the eagle, or the owl that you thought you were? You're just a sheep. And you need a shepherd. Not just any old shepherd. But a good shepherd. One who will save you from the wolf of God's judgment.

✤   ✤   ✤

It could be that you are thinking, 'I don't get this. I don't get why Jesus died for me. I didn't ask him to. And I don't really see why he needed to.'

Chapter 10

THE SERVANT KING
John 13:1–17

We will never get hold of the life that Jesus came to bring until we get hold of the death that Jesus came to die. It has been a recurring theme: in John 3 Jesus explained that it was his being lifted up on the cross like the snake on the pole that would bring life to all who believed in him. In John 6 Jesus puzzled the crowd by saying that if they fed on his death they would live for ever. In John 10 he declared that he was the Good Shepherd who lays down his life for his sheep.

By the time we get to John 12, pilgrims from all over the country are streaming into Jerusalem for the Passover Festival. The streets are alive with a cheering, chanting, dizzy crowd, celebrating how God had set them free from slavery in Egypt and rejoicing in the day when God would keep his promise and send his King to set them free once more.

This particular year, there was a group of pilgrims who had arrived breathless from Bethany with the news that they had come across a man named Jesus who had raised their friend Lazarus from the dead. Word spread and fuelled the speculation. Was this Jesus the King who could fix this broken world? When Jesus rides into Jerusalem on a donkey, the crowd, waving palm leaves as we would wave flags at a coronation, hail him as their King. In the gathering excitement, some Greeks track down Jesus. They have picked up the rumours and they want to know what sort of a King Jesus is.

Jesus answers their enquiry by announcing, 'The hour has come for the Son of Man to be glorified' (12:23). He is talking about himself. And he is saying that the time has at last come for God's King to show himself to all the world in all his brilliance. The Greeks must have been a little bemused. The spectacle of Jesus riding in on a donkey would hardly have struck fear into the hearts of the Romans. The rabble that hailed him was no match for the Roman army. What sort of glory was he planning on dazzling everyone with?

Jesus explains:

I tell you the truth, unless a grain of wheat falls to the ground and dies, it remains only a single seed. But if it dies, it produces many seeds. (12:24)

This King is not going to take over the world with tanks; he is going to take over the world in the way that a seed takes over a field. He is going to die. And it is out of his death that his kingdom will grow. That is why he goes on to say:

Now my heart is troubled, and what shall I say? 'Father, save me from this hour'? No, it was for this very reason I came to this hour. (12:27)

In the Millennium Dome in London there was an exhibition that dismissed Jesus as 'a good teacher who died tragically young'. But Jesus says that his death on the cross was no accident. It was the very reason he came. So in John 13 Jesus has taken his close followers away from the hustle and bustle of the crowds and, over the intimacy of a meal, he prepares them for all that must happen to him.
John introduces it:

It was just before the Passover Feast. Jesus knew that the time had come for him to leave this world and go to the Father. Having loved his own who were in the world, he now showed them the full extent of his love. (13:1)

We have heard Jesus talk about himself as the one who has come from the Father, and now he is preparing to return to the Father. He wants his disciples to know that the impending betrayal, arrest, trial and execution are not events that have spun out of his control. The cross is the climax of what he has come to do. It is on the cross that he would show them the 'full extent of his love'. This means that if, today, we want to take in how much Jesus loves us, it is to the cross that we must turn.

It is a puzzling thought. If, when I was walking along the coastal path on Pentire Head in Cornwall, I had turned to my wife and said, 'I want to show you how much I love you' and then proceeded to fling myself off the edge of the cliff,

I think it would be hard for her to see my death as a demonstration of the 'full extent' of my love for her. She might see it as a demonstration of the fact that I was not at all well, but not as a demonstration of my love. Flinging myself off the clifftop would amount to little more than a futile gesture.

But if my wife had slipped and fallen into the sea and I had jumped in after her and helped her to safety, only to be swept out to sea myself, then she might well look back on my death as a demonstration of how much I loved her. In years to come she might be able to say, 'Mike loved me so much that he gave up his life to save me.'

Jesus' death on the cross was not a futile gesture. It achieved something. It rescued us. We had fallen and were in real danger. But in his love he gave up his life to save us.

'But,' you ask, 'how can the death of a man two thousand years ago save us today?' Fair question.

When Jesus raised the paralysed man, it pointed to the fact that he was the one who will raise all people to new life. When Jesus fed five thousand people, it pointed to the fact that he was the bread of life. Now, what he does for his disciples as they sit down for a meal points to what he will do on the cross. It points to *how* his death two thousand years ago saves us today.

THE SERVANT KING

> Jesus knew that the Father had put all things under his power, and that he had come from God and was returning to God. (13:3)

Jesus knows that his Father has given him power over the whole universe. Look at what he does with his power:

> So he got up from the meal, took off his outer clothing, and wrapped a towel around his waist. After that, he poured water into a basin and began to wash his disciples' feet, drying them with the towel that was wrapped round him. (13:4–5)

In Jesus' day, when you arrived as a guest in someone's home, a servant would take off your sandals and wash your feet. When you think of the heat and of all that you might have walked through or trodden in on the way, you can see why this was a job traditionally reserved for the lowliest of the servants. That night, the disciples were a group of men puffed up by the prospect of power. Events were coming to a head. Their leader had declared himself to be the King, and over supper they were jostling for the top jobs in his kingdom. No doubt they were only too aware that there was no servant around to wash their feet, but none of them was keen to step up. When you want to prove to your boss that you are ripe for high-level responsibility, you don't show him how good you are with a mop.

If I had been Jesus, I would have waited until someone else felt shamed into fetching a bowl of water. Kings do not get down on their hands and knees.

But it turns out that this King does. This King has all the power and authority in the universe, and it turns out that he doesn't use it to flatten his enemies, but to get down on his hands and knees and serve us.

The disciples sat in sheepish silence. What is there to say, when your King is cleaning out the dirt from between your toes? The minutes must have dragged on uncomfortably. Jesus has shown them up for what they are: proud men who thought it was beneath them to wash feet. And the same pride that meant Peter wouldn't get down on his hands and knees meant he wouldn't let Jesus do it either.

> He came to Simon Peter, who said to him, 'Lord, are you going to wash my feet?' (13:6)

'This is all wrong,' says Peter. 'You shouldn't be washing my feet. You're the king. I should be serving you. Why are you doing this?'

> Jesus replied, 'You do not realise now what I am doing, but later you will understand.' (13:7)

'You may not understand why I am doing this now, but you soon will,' says Jesus. 'The next time you see me stripped and standing in the place of the lowest of the low, it will be on a cross. And you will think that it is all wrong. But there on the cross you will see the sort of King I am. You will see that I have come to serve you.'

Peter is having none of it and, as he tries to grab the cloth, Jesus explains: 'Unless I wash you, you have no part with me' (13:8). 'You must let me wash you clean. If you don't let me wash you clean you will never be part of my kingdom.'

WE NEED TO BE WASHED CLEAN

As a small boy, I once came home from a blissful morning's pike fishing covered in mud and slime. My mother, who had spent the whole morning cleaning the house, wouldn't let me in through the front door. So I had to go round to the back, where she stripped me off and scrubbed me down before I could step inside.

Before we can step inside God's kingdom, we need to be washed clean.

Our temptation is to think that, if God is so good, he should just fling open the door and let us all come traipsing in. What is his problem with a bit of dirt? But it is precisely *because* he is so good that he has a problem with dirt. 'Dirt' is an image used in the Bible for 'sin'. You and I can live with a bit of sin. But God can't, because God is good. In his goodness he is totally opposed to all that is evil in this world. When we ask him to let us in with our muddy boots, we are asking him to tolerate our selfishness, turn a blind eye to our greed and shrug his shoulders in the face of our lies. In other words, we are asking God to stop being good. Our question is, 'If God is so good, how can he shut us out?' The real question is, 'If God is so good, how can he let us in?' You see, it is precisely because God is good that he will not smile at sin. He will condemn it.

Right from the outset, Jesus has made it clear that he has come on a rescue mission. When you rescue someone it is because they are in danger. Listen to how Jesus describes the danger that we are in.

> Whoever believes in him is not condemned, but whoever does not believe stands condemned already because he has not believed in the name of God's one and only Son. (3:18)

> Whoever believes in the Son has eternal life, but whoever rejects the Son will not see life, for God's wrath remains on him. (3:36)

'Wrath' is a word for God's anger at our sin. Jesus is saying that the danger we faced was God's condemnation. As things stood, God's just condemnation of our sin meant we faced being shut out of his kingdom. But in his love God sent his Son to rescue us. And rescuing us meant rescuing us from his condemnation.

Do you remember what he promised in chapter 5?

> I tell you the truth, whoever hears my word and believes him who sent me has eternal life and will not be condemned; he has crossed over from death to life. (5:24)

Jesus promises that if we believe in him, we 'will not be condemned'. And now, with his flannel and soap, Jesus acts out a parable of how it is that his death on the cross saves us from God's condemnation. We are dirty. We cannot come into his kingdom. So, in his love, what does he do? He stoops down to wash us clean.

But, like Peter, we shrink back. If he had come to call us to keep rules or perform rituals, we like to think that we would have risen to the challenge. But he doesn't ask us to do something for him. He is the King who has come to do something for us. And for proud people like us, that is very humbling. Like Peter, we don't want him serving us, because we don't want to be indebted to him. We don't find it easy to admit that we need someone else to wash us clean.

'Dirty' is not only the *Bible*'s image for what sin makes us. It is how we feel. Because it is how we are. The pop psychologists have told us that our guilt is not real. Yes, there *are* people who labour under the burden of false guilt, but

Jesus is confronting the guilt that we know to be only too real. We've been kept awake at night by it, and woken up early with a heavy heart because of it. In our minds we have replayed the scene a thousand times, and we would do anything to be able to unsay what we said or undo what we did, but we cannot rewind the tape and we cannot erase our guilt. Guilt has a way of making it hard for us to live with ourselves. So we try and push it to the back of our minds and bury it under a heap of mitigating circumstances. But that doesn't work. We long to feel clean again. But nothing we can do or say seems able to wash our guilt away. And

He doesn't ask us to do something for him. He is the King who has come to do something for us.

that is why we need to swallow our pride and let Jesus wash us clean.

JESUS WASHES US CLEAN BY HIS DEATH

We've seen again and again that it is the Old Testament that gives us the lens through which to make sense of Jesus. And if we are to make sense of his death on the cross, we need to look at it through the lens of the Old Testament sacrificial system.

When the people of Israel offered sacrifices in the temple, it wasn't to try and twist God's arm into blessing them. The sacrificial system was God's good gift to his people. He had taught them that before they could come into his presence, they would need to be cleansed of their sin. And it was through this sacrificial system that he made them clean.

In one of the most important sacrifices of the year, the people would all acknowledge that their sin meant that they faced God's condemnation. The priest would then take two young goats. One of the goats was killed in order to 'atone' for the people's sins. 'Atonement' is the paying of a price which justice requires. The Hebrew word carries the idea of 'covering' something. After a meal in a restaurant, justice requires that we pay the bill. Our friend might ask, 'Have you got enough money to *cover* the bill?' Once you have 'covered' the bill, it is dealt with and there is nothing more to pay. You can go. Each year the death of the goat 'covered' the people's sins. The priest would then lay his hands on the other goat and say, 'Let our sin be transferred onto this goat.' This goat would be driven out into the desert and would symbolically carry the people's sins far away.

At the end of it all, the priest would pronounce that the people were now clean in God's sight.

If, on your way home from the temple that evening, someone had stopped you and asked how it was possible to come into God's presence, you would have said something like this: 'Our sin means we deserve to be shut out of God's presence. We deserve death. But in his mercy, God provided a substitute to pay for our sin by dying in our place. Our sin means we are dirty in his sight, but in his mercy God has made us clean, because our sin was transferred onto another and carried away into the desert, never to be seen again.'

This sacrificial system was a kind of visual aid. It pointed to the fact that one day God was going to provide one final sacrifice that would both pay the price for our sin and remove it from us once and for all. The day when God would come and finally cleanse them from their sin was a day that God's people longed for. Hundreds of years before Jesus, the prophet Isaiah had looked forward to the great King who was to come and set God's people free. But his is an intriguing portrait of how the great King would come as a servant – a servant who would serve his people by dying as a sacrifice for their sins.

> Surely he took up our infirmities
>   and carried our sorrows,
> yet we considered him stricken by God,
>   smitten by him, and afflicted.
> But he was pierced for our transgressions,
>   he was crushed for our iniquities;
> the punishment that brought us peace was upon him,
>   and by his wounds we are healed.
> We all, like sheep, have gone astray,
>   each of us has turned to his own way;
> and the LORD has laid on him
>   the iniquity of us all.
> (Isaiah 53:4–6)

As we watch Jesus washing his disciples' feet, we are brought face to face with the Servant King that Isaiah was looking forward to. And as we go on to see Jesus die on the cross, we see the full extent of what it meant for him to stoop down and serve us.

His death was no accident. His death was the sacrifice that all the sacrifices in the temple had pointed to. On the cross, he died to pay for our sin. There is nothing more for us to pay. On the cross our sin was transferred onto him and carried away. In God's eyes, we are clean.

A Tale of Two Cities by Charles Dickens is a novel set during the French revolution. Quite early on, we meet Charles Darnay, a French aristocrat, and Sidney Carton, an English lawyer. They are rivals for the same woman. After much toing and froing in the fog between London and Paris, Darnay ends up in the Bastille, facing the guillotine. But Carton finds a way to save his rival. He steals into the Bastille, drugs Darnay, exchanges clothes with him and then stays in Darnay's cell, while a friend smuggles the drowsy Darnay to freedom. The next day, Carton is executed in Darnay's place.

Darnay went free because Carton died his death for him. It is a pale comparison, but what Carton did for Darnay is something of what Jesus came to do for us. His death was not a futile gesture. We were in grave danger. We had defied God and messed up his world. We faced his just condemnation for our sin. But in his love he found a way to save us. He sent his Son into the world, and on the cross the Son of God stood in our place and died our death for us. His death means we can live.

I don't know what you make of a rescue plan like this. It's not one that you or I would have dreamed up in a million years. But it is how God has chosen to rescue us. And the more you think about it, the more amazing it is. Jesus had said that the hour of his death would be the hour of his glory. Now we can see why. In the death of Jesus we see just how good God is: we see his justice and we see his love. We see his justice because, when we look at the cross, we see that God does not ignore our sin. He condemns it to death. And we see his love. When we look at the cross we see that he is more loving than we could ever imagine. Yes, the price for sin has to be paid. But do you see what he does? For our sin, he himself pays the price.

Because God is good, he will not let dirty people like us into his kingdom. But he wants us to have life with him. So he himself comes to wash us clean. It costs him everything. But that is how much he loves us. That is how good he is.

HIS DEATH CLEANSES US ONCE AND FOR ALL

When the penny drops, Peter bursts out with verse 9: 'If I need to be washed in order to be part of your kingdom, then don't just wash my feet – wash me all over!' Jesus assures Peter that his death will wash Peter thoroughly clean.

> Jesus answered, 'A person who has had a bath needs only to wash his feet; his whole body is clean.' (13:10)

As he does with so many of his images, Jesus now uses the image of cleansing in a slightly different sense. He is saying that the cleaning that he will do on the cross will be like having a bath before going out to dinner. When you arrive at your host's house, you may need your feet cleaned up, but you don't need another bath, because fundamentally you are clean.

Some people think that the death of Jesus has wiped their slate clean. They rejoice at the chance of a fresh start. But then it is not long before they mess the slate up again. This leaves them wondering where they stand with God, worrying if he will ask them to leave. But what Jesus is saying is that, once he has made us clean, although our feet will get dirty, because we will trip up into sin and will need to ask God to forgive us, in God's eyes we remain fundamentally clean. It is not just a clean slate that Jesus gives us, but a clean *state*.

In my first job as a junior vicar, I arranged to meet a friend called Simon Weatherseed at his office in the City of London. I set out in an old denim jacket, and over my shoulder I carried a canvas army surplus bag that I had several times rescued from the bin when my wife wasn't looking. It was only when I stood in front of the main door of this huge bank that I realized that I was not appropriately dressed. As I climbed the stairs a large uniformed guard came straight for me and blocked my path. 'Can I help you?' he enquired.

This is a very smart bank. I am dressed like a twelve-year-old, and the guard is suspicious of my intentions. I need to get in to see my friend Simon. What do I do? Do I pull out my library card or my driving licence? Do I tell him about my A-level results? Mention my batting average? Do I reassure him that I am in fact a clergyman in the Church of England? Should I offer to buy him lunch, perhaps? No. There is only one thing that I can say that will get me into the bank: 'I've got an appointment to see Simon Weatherseed.'

Phone calls were made, I was escorted through a series of barriers and Simon and I went for lunch in what was laughingly called the cafeteria. We had monkfish. In my book monkfish is the sort of treat you have on your wedding anniversary. And we had it on an ordinary Thursday for a working lunch. In this dining room full of suits, I was very conscious that I was dressed like a twelve-year-old. And whenever Simon and I became separated because he went to get a fork or something, I found myself nodding at Simon and waving at him and generally trying to make it as clear as I could to all around me that I was with him.

My only hope of getting into that bank was Simon. Nothing else I could say or do could even get me into the lobby. And Simon was not just the only way to get into the bank. In the moments when I felt acutely out of place, Simon was the only way I *stayed* in the bank. Because of him I could relax and enjoy the monkfish.

There is nothing we can do to get ourselves into the presence of God. We may try to scrub ourselves up by going to church and giving to charity, but our only hope of walking into the presence of God is for Jesus to wash us clean. And what he is saying is that his death is not only the reason we can come into the presence of God, but the reason we can *stay* in and enjoy life in his presence. There are days when we will mess up and our sin will make us feel acutely out of place. We will feel that we should leave. But Jesus wants us to know that because of his death we can stay.

What a relief this is. In so many of our relationships we are never quite sure where we stand. If we do well, they love us, but if we mess up, the jury is out. Jesus assures us that if we put our destiny in his hands, then our place before God is totally secure. It is secure because it doesn't all hinge on how well we do. It all hinges on what he has done. He has made us clean once and for all. So, because of *him*, we can stay.

We can stay because God does not do forgiveness in the way that we do forgiveness. Some people *say* that they have forgiven you, but you know that they haven't because they keep dredging your sin back up again and hurling it at you, like mud. But God is not like that. He does not use our sin as evidence against us any more. He has removed our sin from us 'as far as the east is from the west' (Psalm 103:12). Do you see what that means? It means that if we have let Jesus wash us, then when the God of the universe looks at us he won't look on us as dirty. He will look at us with utter delight. Our guilt weighs us down. But when God looks at us he says, 'You are clean.' That is the moment of ultimate freedom that the people of God in the Old Testament longed for.

And that is why Jesus cries out from the cross, 'It is finished' (19:30). He has done what he came to do. By his death he has set us free.

John keeps reminding us that it is Passover time. People were looking forward to the day when God would keep his promise and set his people free. John wants us to look at the death of Jesus and marvel at how God kept his promise.

THE CROSS-SHAPED COMMUNITY

By washing us clean Jesus brings us not just into a new relationship with God, but into a new relationship with one another.

> Now that I, your Lord and Teacher, have washed your feet, you also should wash one another's feet. (13:14)

Jesus is not merely commanding his followers to take a keen interest in one another's personal hygiene. He is calling us to treat one another in a way that reflects how he has treated us. Washing feet is just one example. Rather than using what power we have to put others down, Jesus calls us to use what power we have to serve them and build them up.

Just imagine how different life would be if we all lived the Jesus way. We are only too conscious of the fact that whether we are in a seminar, at a party, or waiting outside the school gate, we play the same game that the disciples were playing in that room. In every circle of people, there is an unwritten pecking order that we are so acutely aware of that we walk home worrying about the sort of impression we made and hoping that what we said was funny or clever enough to lift us up a notch or two in the rankings. This is why some of our circles of friends are such lonely places to be. When the culture is so competitive, it is very hard to make ourselves vulnerable to one another by admitting any sign of weakness. So we feel we have to wear a mask and pretend that we are bigger and stronger than we really feel.

But Jesus' death for us changes everything. The cross says that in God's eyes there is no pecking order. We are all in the same boat. None of us is as impressive or as sorted as we try to make out, because we are all dirty on the inside and in desperate need of being washed clean. There is no need to go on pretending any more.

The Christian community is not a community of people who think they are better than everyone else. It is the community of people who have been washed clean. I am painfully aware that Christians like me often come across as people who are annoyingly pleased with themselves. But if Christians like me really took in what Jesus has done for us on the cross, it would melt our pride. The cross shows us how laughable all our posturing is. I am as dirty and as needy as the next person, and the only reason I am in a relationship with God today is because the King has stooped down from his throne and washed me clean. If I took that into my heart, it would change the whole focus of my relationship with other people. You see, the cross gives us a whole new currency to use in our relationships with one another. The old currency was 'me first'. The new currency is 'others first'. So, rather than focusing on myself and worrying about what everyone thinks of me, the cross means that I should focus on you. Instead of seeing you as a rival, I should see you as someone who is in the same boat as I am. Instead of trying to make you feel small, I should do what I can to serve you and build you up.

At this point, you may be nervous that Jesus is calling you to join a community of doormats. But look again at the example that he sets. Jesus is no doormat. There is nobody in the universe with more power than Jesus. What he shows us is the right way to use power. *We* use it to flatten the people who are in our way. *He* uses it to serve the people who are in need. Imagine being part of a community in which, instead of using their energy to put one another down, people used their energy to build one another up. This is the kind of revolution we long for in our society. But it is the kind of revolution that only the death of Jesus makes possible.

By his death, Jesus gives us life. He restores us to the relationship with God that we were made for. But it doesn't stop at that. By his death Jesus also restores us to the relationships with one another that we were made for. That it is why Christianity is not a private spirituality. It is not just 'something between me and God'. It is world-transforming.

✤ ✤ ✤

But how can we ask a dead man to wash us clean today?

Chapter 11

THE FUTURE
STARTS TODAY
John 20:1–31

Christmas is easy. We say it's for the children, because it is all about a baby. And babies are, on the whole, safe. But Easter is a little awkward. It's not really one for the children, because the baby grew up and was murdered. Brutally. And so, with bunny rabbits and chocolate eggs, we turn the events of Easter into a poem about how Mother Nature has not forgotten us. As spring follows winter and chicks hatch out of eggs, hope grows out of despair.

But the death and resurrection of Jesus is not a metaphor. If you had been there you could have watched the soldiers hammer the nails through Jesus' hands and feet. You could have stood in the crowd as the cross was lifted up and seen Jesus fight for breath as he pushed up against the nails in his feet only to wrench his arms as he collapsed back down again.

You could have witnessed the moment when they twisted the spear into his side to make sure that he was dead. If you had waited around, you could have followed Nicodemus and a man called Joseph of Arimathea and watched them as they wrapped Jesus' body in spices and strips of linen. They might have asked you to help them lay the corpse in the cool of the tomb and heave the stone across its entrance.

One of the reasons we cover Easter in chocolate and metaphor is because the events that took place are not safe. They change everything.

WHAT HAPPENED?

Jerusalem was throbbing with Passover celebrations. But, as the holiday got into full swing, for the friends and family of Jesus it had been a long and lonely weekend. They had watched Jesus condemned and crucified. And it was not just that they had lost someone they loved, it was that all their dreams had been shattered.

The things he had done and said had made them dare to think that he was the King whom God had promised. At supper with his friends, he'd said he had to go away to die, and that his dying would put everything right. But it didn't. It just made everything all wrong. You see, the King whom God had promised was going to conquer death. 'Death would not be able to hold him' is what one of the ancient writers had said. Jesus' body was now lying cold in the grave. He couldn't possibly be the King. Not now. All that was left for them was to get out their nets and go back to their fishing.

But just a few weeks later, Peter and the others stood up on the steps of the temple in Jerusalem and proclaimed to a crowd of thousands that Jesus, the man whom they all saw crucified, really was God's King.

What had happened to turn them around?

The tomb was empty

I guess Mary found it hard to get any sleep that night. She and some of the other women probably thought, 'We're so wide awake, we might as well get up and go and finish tidying up at the tomb.' So, early on Sunday, they set out. John says that when Mary got to the tomb 'it was still dark' (20:1). In the way that Nicodemus came to Jesus 'at night', it was not just that the sun was not yet up. John is saying that they had no light on the terrible events of the past few days.

When they got there, we read, 'Mary ... saw that the stone had been removed from the entrance' (20:1). She didn't look inside, but she feared the worst, so she raced back to Peter and John (who is the 'other disciple' in 20:2). 'They have taken the Lord out of the tomb, and we don't know where they have put him!' (20:2).

It's the same *they* who dig up the roads, reroute the buses and put up taxes. *They* had taken the Lord. Maybe Peter and John thought it was grave-robbers (which was not uncommon). Maybe they thought it was the authorities, still refusing to let up, even now. So they raced to the tomb.

People often assume that the resurrection of Jesus is just a reworking of an ancient myth. But John's account doesn't read like ancient mythology. Here is a moment in real time (the sixteenth day of the Jewish month of Nisan, AD 33) and in real space (a tomb in a garden on the edge of Jerusalem).

And here are two men running to the tomb, desperate to find out what has happened to the body of their friend. You get the sort of incidental detail that only an eyewitness would notice.

> So Peter and the other disciple started for the tomb. Both were running, but the other disciple outran Peter and reached the tomb first. He bent over and looked in at the strips of linen lying there but did not go in. (20:3–5)

John gets there first and stops to look into the tomb from the entrance. He sees the strips of linen that Jesus had been wrapped in, but he doesn't go in. He hesitates, as you do at the door of your tutor's study. It is open, but you can't see round it, so you are not sure if there is anyone there.

> Then Simon Peter, who was behind him, arrived and went into the tomb. He saw the strips of linen lying there, as well as the burial cloth that had been around Jesus' head. The cloth was folded up by itself, separate from the linen. (20:6–7)

Peter, true to form, comes up from behind and barges straight in. He sees the strips of linen cloth, looks further round the corner and notices the burial cloth that had been around Jesus' head. He sees it lying separate from the other strips of linen, neatly folded. What is strange is that there is no sign of a struggle. If it was grave-robbers, why did they take the trouble to unwrap the body? And so neatly. Why aren't there bits of bandage and spices strewn everywhere?

> Finally the other disciple, who had reached the tomb first, also went inside. He saw and believed. (They still did not understand from Scripture that Jesus had to rise from the dead.) (20:8–9)

Each time the word 'saw' is used in the passage, it gets a little stronger. Now John sees – really sees – what has happened, and so believes. He hasn't yet understood from the Old Testament that Jesus' resurrection should have come as no surprise. At this stage, John is simply cornered by the facts. If all he was looking at was a totally empty tomb, then this could have been nothing more than the scene of a crime. But what he sees is that there is no body, and yet the grave-clothes are still there, set aside neatly as if by someone who had no use for them.

Here is someone 'whom death could not hold'. John looks at the empty tomb and sees that this is not the scene of a crime. This is the scene of a resurrection.

Wearing our twenty-first-century spectacles, we look at the resurrection and want to say, 'Let's not get all hung up about whether the tomb really was empty or not. What matters is that after Jesus was crucified those first Christians obviously had some sort of spiritual experience that gave them the strength to keep going.'

But if the tomb had not been empty, then the first Christians would never have proclaimed that Jesus was God's King. We think that religious truth can be cut free from the events of history. So we say things like 'It doesn't matter if the miracles really happened or not, what matters is what they mean.' But if you were a Jew at the time of Jesus, the truth about what God was doing was the truth about what God was doing *in history*. The Jewish people weren't waiting for a new metaphor to reflect upon. They were waiting for God to act in history and bring his promises to their climax. And, as we have seen, God did not promise merely a new spiritual experience. He promised a whole new creation. The whole understanding of 'resurrection' in the Old Testament was tied to the promise of something physical. This means that God's people were waiting for someone who would rewind death itself, raise people from the dead and restore them to life with God in a world made new. If the tomb had not been empty, if the *body* of Jesus had not been raised from the dead, they would never have used the language of resurrection. That is why John is so keen to assure us that the tomb was empty.

But what turned those first Christians around was more than the fact that the tomb was empty. It was that they had met the risen Jesus.

They met the risen Jesus
John records some of the occasions on which the disciples met the risen Jesus.

Mary meets him in the garden and runs back to the disciples with the news 'I have seen the Lord!' (20:18). Jesus then appears to his disciples:

> On the evening of that first day of the week, when the disciples were together, with the doors locked for fear of the Jews, Jesus came and stood among them and said, 'Peace be with you!'

After he said this, he showed them his hands and side. The disciples were overjoyed when they saw the Lord. (20:19–20)

When the other disciples told him that they had met with Jesus, Thomas, quite reasonably, said, 'Unless I see the nail marks in his hands and put my finger where the nails were, and put my hand into his side, I will not believe it' (20:25). A week later Jesus stood among them again and invited Thomas to touch his scars. John then goes on to record an occasion when Jesus appeared to his disciples by Lake Galilee and cooked them fish for breakfast over a fire.

It is tempting to assume that when the first Christians said 'Jesus lives!' they meant it in much the same way that middle-aged rock-and-rollers today say that 'Elvis lives!' They mean that, even though he is dead, he lives on through his music and so continues to inspire his fans today. But John doesn't want us to read his book and walk away thinking that he is merely saying that Jesus lives on in the memories of his followers. He emphasizes the physicality of their encounters with Jesus (the scars, the fire, the fish) to underline that Jesus was standing among them not as a ghost, but as a dead man who had been raised to life. And just as, when he entered our world, he took on a body like ours, so, as he returns to the Father, he takes on the sort of newly created body that his followers will all one day be given in the new creation.

The church didn't create the resurrection – the resurrection created the church

It is one thing to understand the claim that John is making. It is another to believe it.

I meet a lot of people who think that the story of the resurrection is a legend that was built up over time. Christianity, they say, was founded as a simple movement in memory of a good man called Jesus. And then, over the years, the stories about him became more and more inflated, as the early church sought to try and make itself more important. The trouble with that theory is that it doesn't fit any of the evidence that we have about the first Christians. The first Christians were persecuted by both the Jewish and the Roman authorities. If their message had been that 'Jesus was a good man', it is hard to understand why the authorities would have wanted to silence them. But if you think, as the Romans did, that Caesar is Lord, then the message that 'Jesus is the Lord of the universe' is politically dangerous and needs to be squashed. Legends take generations to evolve. But 'Jesus is Lord' was the claim that Peter and the others made from the temple steps just a few weeks after Jesus was crucified.

The first Christians didn't create the resurrection. It was the resurrection that created the first Christians. If there had been no resurrection, there would have been no first Christians. After the crucifixion, there was no way that Jesus' followers were even remotely contemplating starting a new movement dedicated to his memory.

In the first century there were many people who claimed to be the Messiah. One of them was Simon bar-Giora. He claimed that he was the king who had come to show the Romans that the God of Israel was mightier than Rome. But Simon and his men were flattened by the Romans. Like Jesus, Simon was executed as a public demonstration of the power of Rome. Imagine two or three of Simon's followers hiding in a cave, for fear of their lives, and one saying to another, 'You know, I think Simon really was the Messiah. There was just something about him...' How do you think his friends would have reacted? They would have told him to stop being so blind. The Messiah was supposed to be more powerful than the Romans. He was supposed to reign over God's new kingdom. But Simon was dead and buried. His mission had come to nothing. He had failed. Best to forget all about him. And so they did.

And that is exactly what Jesus' followers felt after they had watched their leader being crucified. To stand up and claim that Jesus was, after all, the King of the universe would have been laughable. Peter was so embarrassed to be associated with Jesus that just a few hours after Jesus' arrest he denied he even knew him. The crucifixion meant that Jesus was just another one of the scores of people who had promised so much, but then come to nothing.

But something happened that meant they couldn't go back to their fishing. Something convinced them that God was fulfilling his promises of old and that the crucified Jesus was in fact God's King. On that first Easter Sunday, God did something that changed everything. And he did it not just in the hearts of the disciples, but on the stage of world history. He raised Jesus from the dead. The Jesus of Nazareth whom we meet in the pages of John's Gospel is alive today. And Christians today are not people who have been inspired to dream the dreams of Jesus of Nazareth. They are people who have met him.

WHAT DOES THE RESURRECTION MEAN FOR US TODAY?

Jesus is who he said he was
By the time Mary gets back to the tomb, Peter and John have gone home. She finds herself alone, crying. It is not just that she is grieving, but that her grief has been violated. Just as you and I would be, she is desperate to know what has happened to the body of the friend she has lost.

> ... she turned round and saw Jesus standing there, but she did not realise that it was Jesus.
>   'Woman,' he said, 'why are you crying?' (20:14–15)

What a strange question that is. When you see someone crying in a graveyard, you don't need to be Sherlock Holmes to work out why. But here is the first tomb in the history of the universe where tears are out of place. Jesus goes on: 'Who is it you are looking for?' (20:15). '*Who* is it you are looking for?' That is the question Jesus wants her to face up to. And that is the question he wants us all to face up to. *Who* are we looking for? As, like Mary, we try to make sense of what has happened, what sort of a Jesus do we think we will find? Who do we think he is?

It never occurred to Mary that the man standing behind her at the entrance of the tomb could be Jesus. The last time she'd seen him, he had been battered and broken. She watched them take him down from the cross. Then he says her name. And she recognizes his voice. It's him! It's Jesus!

Notice that he has not staggered up to her bleeding heavily and in need of urgent medical help. He is not standing there as a man who has had a narrow escape from death. He is standing there as a man who has conquered death. He has not merely revived. He has been raised from the dead, never to die again. And Mary's grief is turned to joy. Jesus is alive.

But everything is different. Jesus says, 'Do not hold on to me, for I have not yet returned to the Father. Go instead to my brothers and tell them, "I am returning to my Father and your Father, to my God and your God"' (20:17). The Jesus Mary was looking for was Jesus their teacher, Jesus their great friend. Jesus is telling her not to cling on to him as though he has just come back to go on being their teacher and their friend. He explains why: 'for I have not yet returned to the Father'.

Throughout his Gospel, John has been underlining the fact that Jesus is the Son of God, who has come from the Father. Jesus had told his disciples that the time had come for him to return to his Father and take his rightful place on the throne of the universe. They had got their hopes up. But those hopes were quickly buried when his body was laid in the tomb.

The message Jesus wants Mary to take to the others is this: 'Tell them that I am returning to my rightful place.' In other words, 'Tell them that I am who I said I was.' The Jesus we think of as the baby in the manger, or the wandering teacher, or the man who was tragically crucified between two thieves does in fact belong on the throne of the universe. The resurrection means that Jesus is God's King.

When Thomas sees the scars, he sees what the resurrection means and calls Jesus 'My Lord and my God' (20:28). That is exactly the conclusion that John wants us to come to, as we brush against the events of the first Easter.

Jesus has done what he said he had come to do

In the opening chapter of his Gospel, John told us that Jesus came to give us 'the right to become children of God' (1:12). Listen again to the message that he tells Mary to take on to the others: 'I am returning to my Father and your Father, to my God and your God' (20:17). He is saying, 'My Father has become *your* Father.' In other words, he wants them to know that the cross was not a failure. It was a success. He has done what he said he had come to do: by his death he has restored his followers to the relationship with God that they were created for.

Let me pull this together with a slightly foolish story. Imagine that you are exploring in some remote jungle and are captured by some locals. They say that if you want to go free, you must first fight the lion that lives in the cave on the edge of the village. If you defeat the lion, then in honour of your bravery, they will set you free. You have no choice, so you pluck up your courage, roll up your sleeves and begin the slow walk to the cave. As you near it, a little man jumps out from behind a bush and says, 'Tell you what, I'll fight the lion for you. I am Leonard the world-famous lion-fighter. I'll kill him with my bare hands.' It has to be said, it looks unlikely, but you will try anything. So off he goes, down into the cave. For as long as he is in the cave, you don't know if he is who he says, or if he can do what he says he can do. He could just be mad. For as long as Jesus stays in the tomb, we don't know if he is who he says he is, or if he can do what he says he can do. He could just be mad.

As soon as Leonard emerges from the cave, dusting down his shirt and dragging the lion behind him, you know that you can trust him. And you know that, because of him, you now have a future. The fact that Jesus emerged from the tomb shows that we can trust him: he is who he said he was and he did what he said he had come to do. And, because of him, we now have a whole new future.

The resurrection means we have hope for the future

We are people who are trapped by the past and who have no hope for the future. But the resurrection has changed everything. It is not just that the eternal destiny of those who follow Jesus is different. It is that the eternal destiny of the whole universe is different. God has kept his promise to his creation. He has made a new start. And being a follower of Jesus means that we are in on God's new start. We are part of the plan. It is all heading towards the day when we too will be raised as Jesus was, when death will be banished and everything will be made brand new. The resurrection means it is not just wishful thinking. It is like seeing the first daffodils of spring. There may yet be some wintry days, but when we see the daffodils we know that there is no going back. The year is heading towards the summer. The resurrection says that God has started to restore his creation. He has begun by restoring us to himself. And although we may yet have to endure some cold and wintry days, the resurrection means that there is no going back. We are heading for the eternal sunshine of a world made new.

The resurrection means that today matters

Those who follow Jesus are not sitting around waiting to leave this world and 'go to heaven'. They are waiting for the King, who will come back to his world and make it new. That means it is not just that the future is different. It means that *today* is different. The resurrection means that all that we do in this world is not going to be undone by death. Because the King will bring justice, justice matters today. Because the King will bring harmony, the way we treat people matters today. Because the King will renew the creation, caring for the planet matters today. Waiting for the King means living for the King.

And living for the King starts today.

✛ ✛ ✛

Think back to the whales on Darlington beach. If we have put our life in Jesus' hands, he has lifted us off the sand. He is easing us back into the ocean. We are not yet out in open water. But he will not leave us floundering in the shallows of this broken world. He will see the rescue plan through to its completion and will restore us to the ocean, where we will swim once again. But even as he leads us through the shallows, we can feel the surge of the ocean lifting us up. On the beach we were dead. But now we have life. Real life.

SUGGESTIONS FOR FURTHER READING

On the tension between atheism and morality:
Ravi Zacharias, *Can Man Live Without God?* (Nelson, 2004)
John Gray, *Straw Dogs: Thoughts on Humans and Other Animals* (Granta, 2002)

On the Bible:
Amy Orr-Ewing, *Why Trust the Bible?* (IVP, 2005)
Paul Barnett, *Is the New Testament Reliable?* (IVP, 2003)

On the historicity of Jesus:
Paul Barnett, *The Truth about Jesus: The Challenge of Evidence* (Aquila, 2000)
N. T. Wright, *Who Was Jesus?* (SPCK, 1992)
Craig A. Evans, *Fabricating Jesus: How Modern Scholars Distort the Gospels* (IVP, 2007)

On the meaning of the death of Jesus:
Mark Meynell, *Cross-Examined: The Life-changing Power of the Death of Jesus* (IVP, 2005)

On the resurrection of Jesus:
Daniel Clark, *Dead or Alive: The Truth and Relevance of Jesus' Resurrection* (IVP, 2007)

On what it will mean to live for Jesus in every area of our lives:
Julian Hardyman, *Glory Days: Living the Whole of your Life for Jesus* (IVP, 2006)
Vaughan Roberts, *Distinctives: Daring to be Different in an Indifferent World* (Authentic, 2000)